Resource-based Learning

EDITED BY
SALLY BROWN
BRENDA SMITH

**KOGAN
PAGE**

Published in association with the
Staff and Educational Development Association

The Staff and Educational Development Series
Series Editor: Sally Brown
Assessing Competence in Higher Education Edited by Anne Edwards and
    Peter Knight
Assessment for Learning in Higher Education Edited by Peter Knight
Enabling Student Learning: Systems and Strategies Edited by Gina Wisker and
    Sally Brown
Research, Teaching and Learning in Higher Education Edited by Brenda Smith
    and Sally Brown
Resource-based Learning Edited by Brenda Smith and Sally Brown
The Management of Independent Learning Edited by Jo Tait and Peter Knight

SEDA is the Staff and Educational Development Association. It supports and encourages developments in teaching and learning in higher education through a variety of methods: publications, conferences, networking, journals, regional meetings and research – and through the SEDA Fellowship Scheme. Further details may be obtained from: The SEDA Administrator, Gala House, 3 Raglan Road, Edgbaston, Birmingham, B5 7RA. Tel: 0121 440 5021; Fax: 1021 440 5022; E-mail: office@seda.demon.co.uk

First published in 1996

Kogan Page Limited
120 Pentonville Road
London N1 9JN

British Library Cataloguing in Publication Data

A CIP record for this book is available from the British Library.

ISBN 0 7494 1932 6

Typeset by Kogan Page
Printed and bound in Great Britain by Clays Ltd, St Ives PLC

Contents

The Contributors

Dorothy Bell is Information Assistant in MARCET within the Educational Development Service, University of Northumbria at Newcastle.

Sally Brown is Educational Development Adviser, University of Northumbria at Newcastle.

Tina Carr is Information Officer in MARCET within the Educational Development Service, University of Northumbria at Newcastle.

Andrew Charlett is Principal Lecturer in the Department of Built Environment, The Nottingham Trent University.

Graham Gibbs is Head of the Oxford Centre for Staff Development, Oxford Brookes University.

Charley Hardwick is Information Team Manager in the Library and Information Service, The Nottingham Trent University.

Bernard Lisewski is Principal Lecturer, Liverpool John Moores University.

Leslie Mapp is Director of Programmes for the Open Learning Foundation.

Phil Race is an independent learning consultant, currently working at the University of Northumbria at Newcastle.

Chris Rust is Principal Lecturer in the Educational Methods Unit, Oxford Brookes University.

Eileen Elliott de Saez is Senior Lecturer in the Department of Information and Library Management, University of Northumbria at Newcastle.

Amanda Scott is Business Manager of Pba Training Services, Birmingham.

Chris Settle is Senior Lecturer in Biological and Earth Sciences, Liverpool John Moores University.

Nick Slope is Resource-based Learning Manager, Thames Valley University.

Brenda Smith is Teaching and Learning Quality Manager, The Nottingham Trent University.

Mary Thorpe is the Director of the Institute of Educational Technology, The Open University.

James Wisdom is the Head of Educational and Staff Development, London Guildhall University.

Chapter 1

Introducing Resources for Learning

Sally Brown and Brenda Smith

The term 'resource-based learning' is a broad one, encompassing a wide range of means by which students are able to learn in ways that are on a scale from those that are mediated by tutors to those where the students are learning independently.

Resource-based learning is not new. Wags will tell you that they have been using resource-based learning materials to promote learning for years, called books! In reviewing available media for resource-based learning, we will not be ignoring books, which will continue to be the most significant learning resources our students use for the foreseeable future. In recent years, however, there has been an increase in use of media including:

- open learning materials
- study guides
- textbook guides
- workbooks
- video and tape packages.

More recently still, technological developments have made it possible for us to provide our students with many more sophisticated media including:

- computer-based learning packages
- computer conferences
- CD-ROM, multimedia
- computer-mediated discussion groups
- interactive video discs
- materials on the World Wide Web
- teleconferencing, video-conferencing and telematics.

Higher education providers in the UK are increasingly turning to resource-based learning as a means of coping with the conflicting demands to produce ever higher standards of curriculum delivery when, at the same time, conditions of work for both students and staff are declining, for well-rehearsed reasons.

The Higher Education Funding Council for England (and parallel councils in Scotland and Wales) are placing great emphasis on institutions' ability clearly to demonstrate that teaching is undertaken in systematic, productive and efficient ways, with a focus on the students' needs. They want to see that specified learning outcomes contained in the course or module descriptors are demonstrably available to students on their learning programmes. One way to make this visible is by the production of learning resources in which everything is clearly specified. The onus is then on the students to demonstrate learning, rather than on the teaching team to show what has been delivered.

Resource-based learning is also valuable in helping tutors to cope with the diversity of student need. When curriculum delivery is principally available at set times and in set places, the opportunities for students with jobs, forwarding commitments, mobility problems and so on to commit themselves to advanced study are limited. Resource-based learning at its best provides ways for students to learn at their own pace, at all times of the day, often in locations convenient to them, and it also provides back-up for absentees.

Resource-based learning works well when:

- there is institutional commitment to the strategy at the highest level, with realistic expectations of what can be achieved within the timescale on resource limits. The most important aspects of this are covered in Chapter 2;

- academics, librarians, technicians, computing services staff, designers and administrators work together as a team to produce learning materials. Teams on such tasks don't just form by themselves: they need systematic development and maintenance. It is wise to recognize that once a learning curve has been climbed by the group, it is a shame to waste their experience, as is often the case when there is little continuity of personnel in resource-based learning design teams. The chapter on staff development highlights support that is available to staff in this area;

- resource-based learning teams recognize that materials are not just knocked together. Effective design requires specialist abilities which may need to be developed. There is a complex formula for developing learning resources which involves adding subject knowledge to design and layout skills, plus expertise in writing in user-friendly language, the ability to understand learning theory, and to use effective evaluation skills. This does not come cheap, nor does it come quick!

- there is a recognition that materials have a relatively short shelf-life, with the need for continuous improvement;

- the production of materials is properly costed. Disasters occur when, for example, academics are directed to produce them in their own time, or when reprographics are skimped or rushed. We would do well to emulate the practice of the Open University where design teams work to well-specified briefs which are carefully budgeted in advance;

- there is full evaluation by the students involved of the processes as well as the materials used which feeds back in a quality loop into the curriculum design and redesign processes.

CRITICAL SUCCESS FACTORS

Induction – to the resources for staff and students

You and your colleagues need a clear shared vision of the reasons why resource-based learning is being used and how to make it work well. Without induction, it is common for staff to fail to understand the use of resource-based learning materials to replace rather than supplement existing delivery mechanisms. Students also need clear briefing to ensure they know what is expected of them and why.

Managing students' access to the resources if they don't each have their own

A common refrain from tutors is that students don't buy books anymore. This is hardly surprising, given the financial constraints many struggle under. At the same time it is recognized that libraries too are under pressure. Whereas the average spend per student on books in a university library in the UK ten years ago was four books, now it is one. If students can't get hold of books from the library and have few of their own, we can no longer rely on their ability to read widely around the subject. In this kind of situation, tutors have to adopt creative solutions, so that those few available resources are spread around evenly and that technological solutions are embraced whenever possible.

Study skills development

Many tutors have identified the difficulties associated with using resource-based learning with the so-called 'professional student' (as described by Pauline Kneale, forthcoming); that is, the student who is studying for a degree or a diploma because alternative careers are unattractive or unavailable. It is hard enough to motivate such students to put energy and effort into conventional study, let alone to develop the degree of commitment and independence that resource-based learning requires. If such students see the movement from high class contact hours to greater emphasis on self-study as a reduction of their necessary workload, then severe problems can arise. These students will need detailed and possibly very directive briefing to ensure that they get the most from their studies. Phil Race, in Chapter 3, indicates the particular kinds of study skills support which may need to be implemented.

Appropriate learning activities – which make students engage with the resources

Students need to be prompted to engage effectively with the resource-based learning materials provided, which means that each element needs to provide opportunities for interaction. It is good practice, when reviewing resource material, to keep asking the question, 'What is the student doing now?' If the answer is always 'reading' then the chances are that the learning gain by the student will be limited. We cannot just fling information at them on the page or on the screen and expect them to make sense of it all, any more than we can when they are passive receptors in the traditional lecture hall. They need to be writing, thinking, researching, questioning, reviewing, envisioning, synthesizing, evaluating, analysing, practising, explaining, imagining, proposing – in short, doing (*pace* Race, 1994).

Student support systems – surgeries, group work, seminars

Once some proportion of curriculum delivery is transposed from class contact periods to resource-based learning, other ways of using staff/student interactions can be evolved. If the pressure to 'get through the curriculum' is eased, tutors can use the remaining time available with students to fill gaps, enable theory to be put into practice, answer questions, support those who are struggling, stretch those who are soaring and contribute to the whole learning process. Some of the time previously given over to lecturers can then be used for surgeries, where only those who need help see tutors individually or in groups by appointment, or for seminars where the students can participate more actively.

Frequent feedback built-in

Many would argue that feedback is a principal instigator of learning. One of the problems of much unsophisticated resource-based learning is that students aren't helped sufficiently, frequently or thoroughly to know how they are doing. Resource-based learning must then build in mechanisms by which students can continuously check how much they are learning so they can remedy deficiencies and correct errors as well as integrate new learning into existing frameworks.

Appropriate assessment strategies which support students' learning

If you change the curriculum delivery strategy but don't change the assessment methods, problems can ensue. Assessment methods that rely heavily on information recall, such as traditional exams, cannot test many of the skills and abilities developed by resource-based learning, and assessment that is end-point rather than continuous may well also be of lesser value. Tutors using resource-based learning must face the challenge of devising an assessment strategy that maximizes the skills and knowledge that students have developed, which will tend to include such methods as case studies, in-tray exercises, assessed seminars, presentations and open-book exams (Brown and Knight, 1994).

Evaluation and refinement of the materials

It is a mistake to think of resource-based learning materials as being set in stone. On occasions, tutors and teams consider their work over once a package is completed, whereas, in fact, it is often just beginning. The best resource-based learning materials are dynamic, being regularly reviewed and updated, particularly in the light of feedback received from students who have used the materials. We ignore this at our peril. The only thing worse than resource-based learning materials that are released too early onto unsuspecting students before piloting and trialing is complete is the use of packages that are dated and inaccurate. Mary Thorpe develops this further in Chapter 13.

PERILS TO AVOID

Overloading the students

Our natural desire to provide students with all they need can result in the inclusion of far too much material for them to digest. A good practice for producers of resource-based learning material to adopt is to work through the materials themselves, in the certain knowledge that the time they take is likely to be shorter than their prospective users. Realistic estimates of potential student achievement can also be obtained by trialing and piloting elements of a package with selected groups of students.

Over-emphasis on content

The least effective packages around are those where the tutors have simply bundled up together every handout ever used in the department, with no linking sections and no tasks for students. Tutors do better to provide slimmed down packages that students can really use, rather than providing them with information overload in the form of telephone directory-sized packages.

Material that is dated in content and form

Cruel jokes are made about the fashion wear of Open University presenters on programmes made ten or more years ago. It simply isn't possible totally to avoid in-built obsolescence, but the producers of resource-based learning materials would do well to continually ask themselves whether their material will go out of date quickly. This will apply not only to the images in the media used but also to the examples, facts and figures and bases of case studies.

Using expensive media which can't easily be updated

The opportunities to use CD-ROM, multimedia, interactive video and so on are potentially huge, but producers need to be conscious of the dangers of commitments to technologies that become obsolete once a major investment has been made. Educationalists who made a heavy commitment to BetaMax video technology come to mind, as does the current debate involving PC and Apple Mac configurations.

Forgetting to build in human contact

Students are becoming less reliant on tutors for information-giving but they still need human contact to support their learning. The role of the tutor has changed over the years and is likely to continue to do so. Ways in which we can be useful to our students include:

- guiding them about where to turn for information
- helping them to find the right questions to ask
- trouble-shooting when they get into difficulties
- encouraging them when they are failing
- enabling them to interact in group work
- inspiring them through our own enthusiasm for the subject
- helping them to apply theory to practice
- updating them on recent developments in the field
- stretching them to develop their full potential.

The interaction we have with students is crucial in helping them to keep motivated and wanting to learn.

Constraining the student experience

The best independent learning systems allow students to range freely across subject boundaries, discovering and following their own areas of interest, setting their own goals and devising their own learning programmes. A danger some foresee in the use of resource-based learning is that we direct students towards a convergent range of materials and activities, rather than promoting divergent approaches. Learning programmes that over-direct students, causing them to work screen-by-screen or page-by-page through preordained and predigested materials are stifling. We need to ensure that the resource-based learning materials we devise enable students to demonstrate their diversity, creativity and originality, or else they are no better than the worst forms of tutor-centred learning.

OPPORTUNITIES OFFERED BY RESOURCE-BASED LEARNING

Overcoming lack of access to lecture theatres, drawing studios, etc

Most universities in the UK are experiencing shortages of teaching accommodation, but few will dispense with classroom teaching all together. However, resource-based learning can offer some remedies when space is at a premium, with self-study packs being used by students for independent learning. Introductory packs on fabrics, for example, are being used at Surrey Institute (Wilks and Gibbs, 1994) replacing some studio-based activity, and workbooks are being used widely instead of some lectures at the University of Northumbria.

When designing learning programmes, we need to be aware that we cannot rely on students having comfortable, warm and convenient places to study in their own homes. For this reason, universities that redesign their curriculum delivery methods also need to rethink their accommodation strategies, especially perhaps by providing faculty-based learning resource centres, as at The Nottingham Trent University.

Providing feedback no longer supplied through tutorials

Few universities in the UK are sufficiently well-financed nowadays to provide one-to-one feedback to students in tutorials. Studies suggest (Race, 1994) that students learn most effectively when they can get feedback quickly, before they lose interest in and familiarity with the tasks they have undertaken. Resource-based learning often includes in-built feedback mechanisms, for example, within text in the form of responses to self-assessment questions or on screen in computer-based systems, with prompted responses on incorrect answers as well as validation of correct ones. This can never fully replace the intimacy of direct feedback, but can frequently be more readily provided.

Providing core learning resources

Where learning resources are in short supply, resource-based learning materials can plug some of the gaps. Making books available, providing copyright-cleared materials in course readers and collecting together core materials in a central location can be invaluable. Creative and innovative ways can be found to build learning resource collections. For example, colleagues can be asked to donate unwanted offprints of journal articles they have written, inspection copies of books they have received, useful papers they have collected at conferences and relevant trade literature. Often this kind of material lies gathering dust in staff rooms, and liberating them for student use can be very helpful. This is not, however, a justification for the jumble sale approach to resource-building. Selection, indexing and managing of resource material must be done well.

A word of caution must be offered here about copyright: in the HEFCE-funded resource-based learning project, the project team often came across frightening examples of abuse of copyright, particularly photocopied material for which permission had not been sought. Copyright law is a minefield as it depends largely on case law: our best advice is for tutors building course learning resource collections to consult their university solicitors or copyright advisers for clarification of what the university recognizes as being permitted.

We would also stress the need for security. In the University of Northumbria at Newcastle we have an excellent resource room in the Department of Built Environment which is plagued by stock losses, despite careful supervision. Resource-based learning rooms cannot just be filled and abandoned: to be effective, they need staffing and maintaining in a systematic manner. This theme is discussed further in Chapter 12.

Information provided for students is more consistent

Inevitably a learning strategy that employs resource-based learning requires a great deal of advance planning, and an advantage of this is that all concerned have an overview of the programme of learning. A corollary of this is that staff should thereby be more consistent in the information they provide for students.

Developing student independence

Students who learn actively tend to develop learning techniques which enable them to become lifelong learners; they are able to choose their own modes of study, pace themselves and evaluate their effectiveness. The best resource-based learning materials can be of benefit here in helping students to take responsibility for their own learning needs.

Improving student learning by encouraging a deeper approach

Where students engage in the interrogation of learning resources in an active way, they are likely to develop deeper approaches to learning than other methods that rely primarily on information-transfer modes.

Improving student participation at seminars

Resource-based learning can be helpful in encouraging students to be more active in seminars when students are given preparatory tasks to be undertaken in advance of the event. Many of us will have experienced ghastly seminars where one student reads aloud a paper which is then discussed in a desultory fashion by a few of the other students who have done a little preparation. The tutor then attempts to bring it all together and often ends up giving a subsidiary lecture. To avoid this, structured tasks can be given to be performed prior to and during the seminar to ensure that students all have something to contribute at the time of the discussion.

HOW THIS BOOK CAN HELP

Resource-based learning can be of enormous benefit to students and staff when it is effectively designed, but it can also be disastrously problematic when it is mismanaged (see Graham Gibbs' cautionary tale in Chapter 2 for an illustration of what this can mean). This book is designed to help tutors and managers to design learning resources that really do help learners to learn and to do so in effective and efficient ways. We hope its value will be to promote a better understanding of what resource-based learning can and cannot achieve, to identify and discuss directions for new developments and to help those initiating resource-based learning in their own institutions to avoid some of the worst identified pitfalls and to benefit from the positive experiences of others.

REFERENCES

Brown, S and Knight, P (1994) *Assessing Learners in Higher Education*, London: Kogan Page.
Kneale, P (forthcoming) 'The rise of the professional student: how can we adapt to cope?'
Race, P (1994) *The Open Learning Handbook* (2nd edn), London: Kogan Page.
Wilks, M and Gibbs, G (1994) *Course Design for Resource-based learning: Art and design*, Oxford Centre for Staff Development.

Chapter 2

Institutional Strategies for Implementing Resource-based Learning

Graham Gibbs

INTRODUCTION

Consider the following account of a mythical degree programme run by a well-established and respected institution, and one lecturer's attempts to introduce resource-based learning.

Over the past decade the average number of teaching hours on courses have halved, from about 50 per cent of total student learning time to about 25 per cent. This means that each hour of teaching, instead of supporting one hour of independent learning, now has to support three hours. The teaching hours that remain to support three times the quantity of independent learning take place in classes which are on average 70 per cent larger than a decade ago. The largest course has nearly three times as many students as a decade ago. Some courses no longer have seminars and those that do have much larger seminar groups – up to 24 per group. These groups are often taught by part-time lecturers or postgraduate teaching assistants. One-to-one tuition has been abandoned. The amount of library or other learning space available to students for them to undertake this increased proportion of independent study has declined by 30 per cent over the decade – and it was inadequate ten years ago. The doubling of the cost of new books and the trebling of the cost of journals has led to reduced acquisitions, cancellation of journals and much lower availability of reading material to support all the independent learning. The chance of books and articles on the reading list actually being available to students in the week they are needed are slim, and students have given up looking. The quantity and quality of feedback on assignments has been greatly reduced and students often do not receive feedback until after the module has finished. Some modules have reverted to exam-only assessment or to the use of multiple-choice question tests in order to cope with the marking load.

In this context a lone lecturer bravely attempts to introduce resource-based learning into a course, believing it to offer a potential solution to many of the learning and teaching problems the degree programme faces. The first thing she discovers is that while she can just about manage to rehash her lecture notes and reading list for a conventionally taught module over the summer, devising materials for a resource-based learning course takes a little longer. The department's duty allocation plan does not involve any development time, assuming that developing courses is a normal part of a lecturer's job. She therefore has to do all the work in addition to her teaching and administration duties. She is only temporarily balked by pressure from the Research Assessment Exercise not to pay 'undue attention' to her teaching, balanced by a Quality Assessment of Teaching visit and, finally, having the course she was preparing learning materials for scrapped at short notice due to 'rationalization'. She is half-way through her second writing marathon when she accidentally encounters someone who has produced resource-based learning materials before and she discovers she is going about it in the slowest possible way.

She then realizes that while library services are free to the department, print-room services are not and that there is even a limit on the print budget for each member of staff, to prevent 'waste', which would restrict any learning package to four pages. The graphics support she needs is separate from the print-room and involves special application forms, to be cleared by her head of department, with no appropriate departmental budget heading and with a six-week waiting list for graphics work. The help she needs with illustrations comes from a third unit in the library. She has to obtain copyright clearance herself, which takes six months the first time she tries, at which point the copyright ground rules change.

The department's word-processing system is incompatible with the system used by the graphics technicians and everything has to be done twice, with editing, proof-reading and corrections being painfully time-consuming. The illustrations librarian isn't computerised at all and in the end desk-top publishing turns into a traditional cut-and-paste job. She becomes quite proficient with 'Letraset'. When she tries to charge students for packages to recover some of the production costs she discovers that this is against the recently introduced Student Charter.

Having overcome all obstacles and actually produced the packages, she discovers that she has nowhere to store the enormous pile which she has to retrieve from the print-room herself, having borrowed some trolleys from the porters. The piles of packages block the corridor, go missing and get damaged. The departmental office refuses to handle the administration of delivering the packages to students, especially as they don't even know who has definitely enrolled until week four and don't like handling cash, and so she spends much of the first two weeks of term in the corridor placating queues of worried students, to some of whom she suspects she has handed at least three packages. Some students claim not to have received a copy of the package right up to week ten. Then she discovers that she can't book the rooms she needs: a lecture theatre every three weeks for administration and testing and a large open space for on-demand tutoring and feedback on tests up to four times a week. Even though her needs are less (and cheaper) than normal requirements, in the interests of 'efficiency' a system has been introduced which involves all courses being allocated one lecture slot a week and one seminar slot per 20 students per week. Any room not used every week will lead to the department being fined by the teaching rooms administration.

The resource-based course involves regular short tests linked to remedial materials and remedial tutorial sessions and two resource-based pieces of course-work. However the university, in the interests of 'economy' and 'maintenance of standards', has instituted a rule limiting coursework to one item per course, with at least 50 per cent of marks coming from an exam. All the resource-based assessment is therefore made voluntary, but as students experience the university system on every other course they don't take the voluntary assignments seriously. Instead, they leave the learning packages in a pile until just before the exam and mug up the night before. They do very badly in the exam.

As part of its quality management system, the department then administers its standard course evaluation forms which include ratings on items concerning 'lectures', 'seminars' and 'reading lists', none of which she uses. Her ratings are inevitably terrible and students complain they did not receive the lectures they have come to expect. The head of department responds by taking the course away from her and allocating it to two part-timers, stating, 'After all, now you have produced the materials any half-decent teacher could run it a lot cheaper'.

She is, of course, turned down for promotion, on the grounds that she devotes too much effort to her teaching, which the ratings show, in any case, to be mediocre.

This may seem a parody, but every part of this sad tale was encountered in one context or another during the 'Course design for resource-based learning' project funded by the Higher Education Funding Council. This project focused on collecting examples of best practice in course design to use new resources in ways which overcame a range of problems associated with increased student numbers, declining resources and strained library facilities. It examined nine subject areas, identifying courses where resource-based learning is used, visiting those involved and collecting detailed case information. It identified a range of different types of resource-based learning and accompanying course designs and sought examples of each for each subject area. The outcome was a series of nine discipline-specific publications (Percival and Gibbs, 1994) and nine national conferences during 1994.

Many of the case studies were presented at these conferences by isolated individuals fighting a hostile and obstructive system. It became clear that while small-scale local innovations could be initiated by enthusiasts, if resource-based learning was going to become widespread and soundly integrated then institutional infrastructures needed to change. Frameworks have evolved (rather than having been designed) over many years in universities and colleges in ways which support conventional course design and delivery based on classroom teaching and library use. Resource-based learning uses teachers, accommodation and learning resources in new ways and many features of institutional infrastructures block developments in resource-based learning.

The project was therefore extended to examine the ways in which institutions can support resource-based learning. This involved undertaking case studies of institutions, through visits, and the examination of documentation, and led to the production of a publication concerning institutional support for resource-based learning (Gibbs *et al.*, 1994) and a national conference. What follows is a summary of the ways in which institutions can support the extension of resource-based learning, based on these case studies.

IMPLEMENTATION STRATEGIES

Institutions are attempting to implement resource-based learning in a variety of ways, none of which are without their own potential pitfalls.

Explicit policy

Some institutions have made explicit policy statements about resource-based learning, have included it in mission statements and have set targets for implementation. The University of Luton, for example, set a target of 20 per cent of all courses being delivered through resource-based learning by 1995/6. It is sometimes assumed that action will follow policy formation, but there may be little control or central support to make implementation swift or comprehensive. The hearts and minds of lecturers and students may be in a different place than those of senior management.

Integration of central support services

There is currently a good deal of large-scale reorganization of those elements of institutions under central control. This can mean the integration of library and other support services such as computing, study skills, educational development, printing, audio visual services, TV studios and print material production facilities. The University of North London, for example, is integrating a range of learner support services in a new 'Learning centre'. While integration may help users, course design and delivery may be largely unchanged and staff from different subcultures, such as librarians, computer centre staff and educational developers, do not instantly change their spots.

Forced change

Some institutions are reallocating key facilities in ways which force change. The most common strategy is the reallocation of teaching space as learning space or learning resource centres so that it becomes impossible to book conventional teaching rooms for conventional teaching. For example, Norfolk College and Wirral Metropolitan College have combined small classrooms into large resource centres, obliging lecturers to change their teaching methods. While such reallocation may produce rapid change it tends to be centrally imposed and may precede staff development or detailed teaching plans to cope with the change.

Pushing single solutions

Some institutions appear to express a commitment to a single solution or technology such as open learning or computer-assisted learning. The visible signs of this commitment include major investment in specialist open learning or teaching technology centres with extensive and sophisticated learning material production facilities and teams of experts. Such centres do not always succeed in engaging teaching staff in comprehensive change beyond a small band of believers and glossy high-profile products.

Bottom-up support

This can include staff development, educational development consultancy, sharing of best practice, reward (such as promotion) for innovation, funding for development projects and improvements in facilities for lecturers to produce their own materials. For example, Oxford Brookes University has succeeded in developing a great deal of resource-based learning without any of the normal institutional support requirements. However, there may be little clear direction and the infrastructure may be unsupportive or even obstructive and as a consequence change may be slow and patchy. The developments at Oxford Brookes have taken 15 years.

Developing students as independent learners

This may involve extended induction programmes, special study skills courses or the kinds of packages on learning skills now being developed at a number of universities such as Sunderland and De Montfort. Unless such initiatives are built in to students' substantive programmes, and unless these programmes reinforce the emphasis on independent learning through their teaching and learning processes and assessment, there may be little productive impact. Generalized learning skills development transfers poorly onto specific courses within varied disciplines.

Devolving budgets and providing course costing information

Some institutions with diverse departmental cultures have adopted the strategy of devolution of responsibility, together with devolved budgets and good management information systems. For example, De Montfort University has developed a system of allocating budgets using performance criteria in a way designed to encourage new course delivery strategies. The intention is that departments become more aware of the cost-effectiveness of their teaching strategies and are in a position to bring about change unhindered, particularly changes involving new uses of learning resources and technologies and less conventional teaching. The link between such budgetary and performance pressures and quality of delivery has not yet been successfully demonstrated.

FEATURES OF INSTITUTIONAL SUPPORT

The features of institutional support described here are not alternatives. Some institutions appear to be failing to support change effectively because they have too few of these features or because individual features are uncoordinated or pulling in opposite directions.

Space for learning

As class contact is reduced, students spend a greater proportion of their time learning independently and they need somewhere to undertake this learning – noisy learning space for cooperative learning as well as traditional silent, solitary library space. There is a chronic shortage of suitable study space; this shortage is much less visible than the shortage of teaching space but no less important. Plymouth and Kingston University libraries have zoned areas offering both silent and noisy, individual and group learning facilities.

The kinds of face-to-face contact necessary to support resource-based learning are often quite different from those used in conventional teaching. They may involve medium-sized workshops or group working sessions, requiring flexible furniture, or consultation sessions in which students work independently or in small groups while a tutor consults with some of the individuals or groups present. Both large, tiered lecture theatres and small seminar rooms may be quite unsuitable in terms of their size, layout and furniture. Inflexible room allocation policies also cause problems.

Some institutions, despite policies of support for resource-based learning, are closing local facilities and collapsing site and subject libraries into large centralized facilities. Centralizing library and other learning resources has bought considerable benefits of security, availability and professional support for the learner using information sources. However, it can separate learning activity from tutor support and learning materials. Some institutions are experimenting with resource areas combining laboratory/workshop/study areas with relevant learning materials and tutor support. To be successful such centres need to overcome the characteristic problems of poor stock records and security and limited staff support and accessibility to students. Norfolk College has developed ten learning resource centres separate from the library.

Incentives for change

In most institutions which count lecturers' teaching hours and attempt to allocate teaching hours reasonably equitably, there is precious little incentive for a lecturer to be efficient. In many cases if someone manages to develop an approach which requires fewer teaching hours they are simply given an additional course to teach to make up their hours to the agreed maximum – in other words, they are punished for efficiency. In this context it is an individual lecturer's personal interest to be as wasteful with teaching hours as possible in order to make their life easier, but at the expense of institutional efficiency. It is possible to reverse this motivational bind by calculating individuals' productivity not in terms of teaching hours but in terms of student learning hours. Counting teaching inputs cannot contribute either to measuring efficiency or producing effectiveness any more than counting inputs to research can measure or improve research productivity.

Developing resource-based learning courses and course materials can be very time-consuming. In the face of pressures to publish and support improved research ratings which exclude practical research into effective teaching and learning, what incentive is there for lecturers to put in this effort? If institutions are serious about encouraging their staff to invest time and effort in developing resource-based learning courses then such accomplishments must be rewarded and be seen to be rewarded.

Course costing

Many course design and course approval decisions are made in ignorance of the consequences of these decisions for costs or cost-effectiveness beyond crude counting of teaching hours. Classroom accommodation costs, assessment costs, the costs of student drop-out and failure, library and laboratory costs and so on are usually ignored, assumed to be impossible to estimate or are charged to other budget headings which departments can ignore. Departments may operate on the assumption that student use of the library is 'free', or that delivering computer-assisted learning is 'free' because the allocation of rooms full of computers and the technicians to maintain them is unrelated to the department's operating budget or is a computer centre problem. Adequate course costing information and devolved budgets are necessary if it is to be demonstrated that, as is often claimed, resource-based learning really is cost-effective, cheaper for the same outcome, or that it improves quality for the same cost.

Course approval and review

Conventional module descriptions, written for course approval purposes, usually describe what is intended to be taught (eg, a syllabus listing or programme of topics) or what teachers do (eg, the number of lectures) but seldom describe what learners need to do in order to learn. A course may be described as a '20-hour' course when this really means a 20-lecture course in which students are intended to study for a total of about 100 hours. It is vital to be clear about what the non-class hours are used for: they usually greatly exceed the class hours and it is the careful planning of the availability of appropriate resources which makes this study possible or effective. Module descriptions also frequently list key readings without any information which would indicate whether students had reasonable access to them. Listing a journal article of which there is only one copy on a module with 200 students would demonstrate inadequate planning. If course approval demanded more careful consideration of independent learning time and the resources to support it, this would greatly encourage resource-based learning.

Course review processes and criteria have in a number of institutions been used to focus attention on issues such as the development of transferable skills by requiring approval or review documentation to demonstrate how the issue is being addressed in each course. In the same way, course review could require attention to be paid to students' access to learning resources or to the adequacy of guidance about how to undertake independent learning tasks.

Materials production

Many lecturers find the simple process of producing learning materials frustrating and obstructive. Many departments still impose tight photocopying restrictions on lecturers, and print-rooms using conventional technology usually cause headaches and delays for lecturers wanting to produce extensive learning packages for large classes or to improve production standards. Institutions seeking to foster resource-based learning have established unlimited, unrecharged print-room budgets to encourage experimentation with learning packages, have made student copying or printing from computers free and have installed electronic systems such as DOCUTEK which allow lecturers to print remotely direct from word-processed files. They have provided graphics support, training in the use of desk-top publishing software and easy access to IT facilities. They have made the loan of video production equipment easy, and supported it with training and open-access editing facilities instead of restricting use to expensive professional studio work.

Production funding

Resource-based learning courses involve a different ratio of design and production to delivery costs than do conventional courses. The writing or rewriting of lectures is considered a normal part of lecturers' duties and is not normally costed separately, and the production of handouts is not normally budgeted for on a course-by-course basis. However, resource-based learning courses can involve substantial design and production costs which are beyond normal budgets. These costs may be recovered over time through more economical delivery, but special arrangements may need to be made to provide for the costs in advance of their recovery. Sometimes large courses undertake five-year business plans in order to explore the costs of alternative delivery strategies, and in some departments a reserve is established to pump-prime resource-based learning development, funded over time through savings in staff and accommodation costs. Many institutions now have central funds of £20k–200k per year open to competitive bidding to support materials development and production projects.

Integrated library and learning support facilities

It is common for institutions' learning support services to operate largely independently of each other. The library may have links with computing, but printing, graphics and audio-visual learning materials production facilities usually operate separately. Human support services such as educational development, staff development and study skills development are usually separate as well. Comprehensive institutional approaches to resource-based learning require coordination of all the services supporting learning. A lecturer wishing to turn a conventional course into an resource-based learning course should not have to negotiate with five separate agencies all with different funding arrangements, priorities, schedules and conceptions of their role. Students needing to find reading material, gain access to a CD-ROM, get study advice, print a course document or produce handouts for a project should not have to trek round the campus dealing with different providers.

Identifying and exploiting existing learning materials

The identification of relevant material has been substantially enhanced by the availability of electronic databases including library On-line Public Access Catalogues (OPACs). Bibliographic software now means that teachers and other staff are able to create personal interest profiles (eg, teaching/learning, research management) which are regularly and automatically run across a wide range of such electronic information sources to build up locally held databases on their PCs. Subsequent applications include the generation of accurate and current reading lists, bibliographies for publication of books and articles, and on-demand reading support material for individual students. This service is available in several British universities and was pioneered at Portsmouth University library. It is a powerful tool in identifying materials for use in resource-based learning.

Licensing arrangements under copyright law permit reproduction of existing materials within the terms of that licence. Most institutions have disseminated information on copyright widely and some have set up copyright clearance units thus providing teachers with a single source of expertise on licence arrangements, 'clearance' for unlicensed material and timescales. A few have used their libraries/resource centres as a means of distribution for resource-based learning materials. An easy line-up between materials identification and availability, copyright clearance, text handling and editing, printing and distribution, is essential to the use of print-based resource-based learning.

Information technology policy and operation

Much IT development to support resource-based learning is undertaken piecemeal, with no coordinating policy or technology standards. Where IT policies exist they are often technology defined and management led. It is less common for them to be determined by learner and teacher support needs. In practice this would mean integration of information sources involving campus-wide information systems, access to local and remote library catalogues, networked CD-ROMs, Internet and so on. ELINOR, a De Montfort University project, is one of a family of 'electronic library' projects currently under development. The aim is to develop a fully electronic library environment within five years. Material in this 'library' would include books, journals and abstracts but also course notes, lectures, overhead transparencies, photographs and diagrams.

Despite more than a decade of use of word-processing, desk-top publishing, databases and e-mail, these basic IT tools are still seldom exploited fully in support of resource-based learning. Few lecturer-owned teaching notes, hand-outs and AV aids are produced using compatible systems to agreed standard styles and they are stored in filing cabinets rather than pooled in electronic databases for easy access and modification by teaching teams or students. Learning material delivery is still almost always via conventionally printed hard copy. Students rarely have electronic access to course information or lecturers' notes and e-mail is rarely used for remote communication between tutors and students. Even where facilities exist, staff development and expert support usually lag well behind and applications tend to be by isolated enthusiasts rather than as a consequence of planned departmental policy and support.

Administration and management information systems

Many structured forms of resource-based learning require better information about student progress, in the absence of informal contact with staff, and better information about use of resources, than is usually available. This may involve computer-based assessment systems which can be used to provide feedback to students or to redirect their effort. It may be necessary to give information to lecturers so that they know what remedial support to offer. It may involve 'swipe' systems so that student use of facilities is logged for assessment or resource management purposes or to recharge users (as at Norfolk College). It may involve automated information-logging systems which trigger tutorial interven-tion (for example after a student has failed two tests or failed to attend lab sessions). Without such information it is possible to lose track of students, and drop-out and failure can increase alarmingly.

Induction and training of students as independent learners

If students are to learn effectively in resource-based learning courses, indeed if resource-based learning courses are to succeed, then they need more and better learning skills than those currently exhibited by students on conventional courses. Well-designed resource-based learning courses with excellent materials can fail if students lack the information-handling skills involving finding, synthe-sizing and using information, and the necessary time and task management skills, etc. It is becoming clear that students need careful and thorough induction into new learning processes, explaining what is expected and how things will operate as well as developing new skills. This may mean a week or two of induction before courses start or additional parallel course components – both features which are difficult to fit into conventional modular course timetable straitjackets. It may mean sets of learning resources about independent learning, as produced by De Montfort University and others. It may mean introductory modules placing a considerable emphasis on learning how to study the discipline in an independent way, with a correspondingly lighter emphasis on content.

Training and support of staff

A number of institutions have indulged in general exhortation or have set targets for the adoption of open, flexible or resource-based learning, without the staff involved even understanding what it is. Staff development is a necessary and sometimes expensive component of change. Staff, including library and support staff, need to understand the nature of resource-based learning and the forms it can take, and to reconceptualize the new roles which different categories of staff need to adopt within resource-based learning courses. Generic training on its own, however, is unlikely to lead to change if staff do not have the necessary technical skills. Designing resource-based learning courses and materials, recasting assessment and support systems and adopting new teaching methods for the remaining student contact all involve new techniques and skills. Many attempts at resource-based learning fail because lecturers simply do not know enough about how to do it properly. One of the most effective adjuncts to training is examples of best practice, especially in one's own discipline. Institutions and the staff development units within them need to make models of best practice readily available: not just examples of well-designed learning materials but details of the operation of the courses which use them.

Lecturers also need time. The first time a lecturer writes a lecture it takes many hours. Over time they get quicker. When lecturers first become involved in writing resource material and designing resource-based learning courses this can take many more hours than conventional course redesign or routine updating of lectures. Over time they will get quicker, but the first time they are involved the additional burdens are so great that without some release from duties it may be impossible. Staff need the time to learn how to teach in new ways. Lecturers also need focused skills-based training. Resource-based learning involves new classroom techniques, new assessment methods and so on, as well as writing and design skills. Such training, however, is difficult to deliver to the right people at the right time and with a sufficiently relevant focus to meet all needs. Usually lecturers need follow-up consultancy: the support of an expert working alongside them while they develop resource-based learning materials and courses, commenting on drafts, suggesting new approaches, obtaining relevant examples and asking evaluation questions.

Evaluation frameworks

Many institutions are now adopting the use of standardized student feedback questionnaires for the evaluation and comparison of courses in the belief that this will assure quality. In fact they can assure uniformity and crush innovation. Many of these questionnaires would automatically lead to poor ratings for resource-based learning courses because they make the assumption that courses are conventional and driven by teaching and, in particular, by lectures. The questionnaire items refer to course features which are missing or not emphasized in resource-based learning courses and omit reference to key features of resource-based learning courses. In such institutions it would be very risky for an individual or a course to adopt resource-based learning, not because it wouldn't work, but because it would appear not to work given the evaluation instrument used. If standard questionnaires were to pay more attention to learning, and to features such as designed provision, availability of learning resources for students and adequacy and appropriateness of library stocks, this would increase pressure to change conventional teaching-dominated courses and review.

Coherence of course philosophies

The 'Course design for resource-based learning' project found that much of the innovation in resource-based learning was being undertaken in isolation from most other teaching, with no coordination of policy. It resulted in students experiencing disorienting variations in course delivery and expectations about what they are supposed to do in order to learn, as well as timetabling and assessment complications. It also caused many frustrating blocks for staff. Some innovation was described as being undertaken despite departmental policy or even in secret. If resource-based learning is to spread and become a mainstream activity it requires departmental coordination which pays attention to issues such as the way expectations of students are communicated and the ways courses are described in documentation.

CONCLUSION

Many of the institutional features listed above are described in the following chapters; some are evident within individual courses or departments rather than having been built into the way an institution operates. They can be used as a checklist for evaluation by institutions. They can also be used by individual lecturers in deciding whether to go ahead with an innovation in resource-based learning despite the context. If too few support features are present, then banging your head against a brick wall might offer a less painful alternative.

REFERENCES

Percival, F and Gibbs, G (1994) *Course Design for Resource-based Learning in Technology*, Oxford Centre for Staff Development.
Gibbs, G, Pollard, N and Farrell, J (1994) *Institutional Support for Resource-based Learning*, Oxford Centre for Staff Development.

Chapter 3

Helping Students to Learn from Resources

Phil Race

Students have always done much of their learning from learning resource materials of one kind or another. It is increasingly accepted that one of the most important outcomes of higher education is that students emerge with well-developed learning skills that will equip them for their future careers and lives. It is therefore important to address students' ability to make good use of the ever-widening range of learning resource materials that they will encounter in higher education. In this chapter, I would like to link together the study skills development that students need, the competence-based frameworks that they are increasingly working within, and the growing diversity of assessment methodology they encounter.

WHAT ARE THE PREREQUISITES FOR SUCCESSFUL LEARNING?

I have discussed elsewhere (Race, 1994) my thoughts and conclusions about this. Briefly, four factors seem to be needed for successful learning. These factors, I believe, remain the same irrespective of the age of learners, their disciplines, and all other elements I have investigated. The factors are:

- *wanting* to learn (motivation)
- *learning by doing* (experiential learning, practice)
- *feedback* (finding out how the learning's going)
- *digesting* (making sense of what has been learned – understanding).

It is thus logical to propose that the effectiveness of resource-based learning depends on these four factors. Since many agree that just about all learning is done through learning resources (especially if we include human tutors as one of the most versatile of learning resources), it is important to give due attention to how best we can help students make the most of learning resources.

WHY DO STUDENTS NEED HELP URGENTLY?

There are several reasons for the urgency of the need to help students become better at learning from learning resource materials.

- We now have larger class sizes in further and higher education, with tighter timetables and overstretched teaching staff.

- As a result of the above, and as a consequence of the information technology revolution, students in many colleges now spend more of their time learning from resources individually.

- With growing recognition of the importance of students developing transferable personal skills, there is more attention to the use of tutorless groupwork, often using learning resource materials.

- The quality and sophistication of many print-based learning resources have increased significantly, and student expectations of learning resource materials have risen accordingly.

- There is growing use of open and flexible learning as part of conventional college-based courses as well as in distance-learning courses, again dependent not only on the quality of learning resources, but also on the extent to which students develop skills at using such resources.

- The dramatic increase in the usage of electronic and computer-based learning systems, including the Internet, adds a new range of learning resources, with corresponding needs for students to become able to learn effectively from them as well as play with them!

WHAT ARE STUDENT EXPECTATIONS?

As indicated above, students expect sophistication and quality in all the different kinds of learning resources they encounter. If a learning package looks homemade and tacky, students don't trust the learning they do from it as much as when it appears professionally produced.

Another factor that affects expectations is the high age-participation ratio of students in higher and further education. Now that around a third of all school leavers enter higher education, it has to be accepted that the student population is significantly different from that which existed in a more elitist education system. One of the results is a tendency towards increased dependence of students on tutors to support their learning. Many students do not think they can have learned something successfully unless they have been *taught* it in some formal way. Yet the overall climate continues to move towards independent resource-based and student-centred learning, and the general empowerment of students regarding their learning.

Further changes which predetermine the nature of the help students need to develop appropriate learning skills arise from the changing nature of assessment of student learning. For example, there are widespread moves (not before time) to diversify assessment, so as not to be limited to written work in formal exam situations or tutor-marked coursework. There is increasing recognition of the importance of student self-assessment and peer assessment, not merely as assessment processes but also as deep-learning processes. Greater attention is also paid to defining not just the intended learning outcomes of courses of study, but also spelling out the nature of the evidence students will be required to furnish in order to demonstrate their achievements.

APPLYING A COMPETENCE-BASED FRAMEWORK TO RESOURCE-BASED LEARNING

Whatever reservations we may have about the use of competence-based frameworks, there is a powerful logic for trying to define and clarify to learners:

- the things they should aim to be able to know and do, when their learning is successful;

- the evidence they should expect to provide, to prove that their learning has been successful;

- the criteria with which the quality of their evidence will be judged, as a measure of the success of their learning.

Such a framework is a learning resource in its own right. It links quite directly with the ways in which students learn, and helps as follows:

- focusing and enhancing the want to learn: learners need to know where the goalposts are, and knowing this helps their motivation develop;

- defining learning by doing: learners need to know *what* they should become able to do;

- drawing attention to the role of feedback: learners need to know how far the evidence they offer of their learning matches the standards required of them;

- setting the scene for the digesting: knowing how they are doing and how much is still to do, are both parts of the process of making sense of, or understanding, what is being learned.

Some of the criticisms of competence-based frameworks vanish if we view them in this way. The argument above does not try to ignore the importance of knowledge and understanding, in a search for the evidence of competence. Furthermore, it is quite possible to build on to such frameworks requirements linked to the demonstration of the upholding of values. Such values may extend far beyond the 'equal opportunities' area often cited, and can include 'pursuing scholarship', 'recognizing individual difference' and 'concern for other people'. In many professions it is increasingly recognized that competence without values is empty. Doctors, nurses, lawyers – and teachers – all need to uphold particular values or ethics to be credible and successful practitioners in their fields. Perhaps the only criticism of competence-based frameworks should be that many of them concentrate too much on evidence of competence, while neglecting evidence of the demonstration of the adherence to relevant professional standards. Perhaps the difference between someone who is merely competent, and some-one who is a professional, lies in the values that the latter can demonstrate as fundamental to practice.

Therefore I would like to direct your thoughts about resource-based learning to:

- the competences that learners need to develop;
- the evidence whereby they will demonstrate their competence;
- the criteria against which their competence will be judged;
- the values upon which such competence should be based.

WHAT STUDY SKILLS DO LEARNERS NEED?

When most learning was done in traditional 'jug and mug' situations, the range of study skills or transferable competences that learners needed was relatively simply defined. Study skills development concentrated on aspects such as:

- note-making skills in traditional lecture situations;

- coursework skills involved in writing essays and reports;

- revision strategies, concentrating largely on how to memorize information which would be required to be recalled and used in traditional formal exams;

- exam techniques which would enable students to perform adequately in the particular skills needed to succeed in formal exams.

It can be argued that the above study skills are still required by students (and also that with the increased participation ratio in higher education, acquiring these skills to an adequate level is an uphill struggle for a greater proportion of students). However, with a diverse range of teaching-learning situations, and a wide variety of learning resources in many different media and formats, students need a correspondingly diverse array of learning abilities. Some of the additional competences that students now need to develop are how to:

- make sense of what learning outcomes really mean in terms of what they actually have to do to achieve them;

- plan and produce portfolios of evidence for assessment;

- take part in self- and peer assessment;

- learn to devise suitable assessment criteria and apply these along with prescribed ones;

- develop appropriate time-management and task-management skills, to accommodate a more varied educational experience;

- develop degrees of autonomy, to allow them to manage their own learning when using resource-based learning, computer-based learning and open and flexible learning pathways.

HOW BEST CAN WE HELP STUDENTS DEVELOP THESE SKILLS?

There are plenty of options available. Which option works best for individuals depends upon their personal learning preferences and the nature of the subject matter that they are learning. Some of the possibilities are as follows:

- large-group study skills presentations
- small-group intensive study skills workshops
- direct guidance as an integral part of subject teaching by the teacher
- printed resource materials on appropriate study skills
- interactive print-based resource materials on study skills
- computer-based study skills development packages
- computer conferencing
- credit-rated study skills modules.

I will next take a brief look at each of these possibilities, illustrating them with things I have learned while trying them out, and listing one or two advantages and disadvantages of each.

Large-group study skills presentations

For many years while at the University of Glamorgan, I offered a series of four 2-hour open evening lectures to students on core study skills matters. In fact, these were not 'lectures' at all, but were highly interactive large-group sessions (usually with around 200–300 students present). In these, it was possible to get students thinking about their own preferred learning approaches, time management, task management, essay writing, report writing, preparing revision tools, planning revision programmes, and exam technique. The sessions were useful for raising students' awareness of their role in handling a variety of resource-based learning environments, and setting them thinking about the approaches they would try out.

Advantages

- It is cost-effective provision.
- There is plenty of opportunity for discussion.
- Students see that their own 'problems' are widely shared.

Disadvantages

- The sessions are necessarily 'general' and it's not possible to go deeply into discipline-related issues.
- One is working with the converted – the students who come along to such 'open' sessions are not necessarily the ones who need help most.

Small-group intensive study skills workshops

Groups of all sizes, working with a tutor, can cover any aspect of study skills development, including all those mentioned above.

Advantages

- Direct discussion and exploration of how best to approach the use of specific learning resources is possible, in the context of particular subjects, topics and courses.
- Students derive a greater sense of ownership of the solutions to their problems, devised in such workshops.

Disadvantages

- It is more costly both in terms of staff time and student time.
- It can be difficult to get the timing right, ie, planning the workshops to coincide with the times when students will commence using particular learning resources.

Direct guidance as an integral part of subject teaching by the teacher

This is, in many ways, the optimum way of helping students develop the most appropriate skills that they need to help them learn effectively from learning resources.

Advantages

- When the guidance is offered by teachers who are subject experts in what students are learning, students see the advice as being authoritative and relevant.
- Lecturers can plan the timing of such guidance to be ideal.

Disadvantages

- It is not possible to motivate all lecturers to provide study skills guidance for students; some think of such help as 'spoon-feeding'.

- Lecturers often feel that the primary need is to get through the syllabus, and regard study skills support associated with making good use of learning resources as a time-wasting luxury that they cannot afford.

Printed resource materials on appropriate study skills

Most study skills texts provide at least some guidance to students on how best to approach using learning resource materials (see, for example, Northedge, 1990; Race, 1992; Saunders, 1994).

Advantages

- Printed resource materials may be inexpensive to purchase (or to photocopy relevant copyright-cleared extracts from).

- This sort of study skills support does not intrude on 'class time', as students can be expected to read the materials in their own time.

Disadvantages

- The guidance from such materials is usually too general to be really useful for students who will be learning from particular resource materials or specific media.

- Students do not get much of a sense of ownership to solutions to their problems.

Interactive print-based resource materials on study skills

Interactive materials (for example open learning packages or self-study workbooks) can address many of the general problems students have in learning from a range of learning resource materials (eg, Bourner and Race, 1995).

Advantages

- Interactive materials can include exercises helping students to become familiar with good ways to approach the use of learning resource materials, and can provide students with at least some feedback on their levels of success.

- Students can select those tasks and exercises which they see as most relevant to particular problems they encounter.

Disadvantages

- Interactive materials are normally bulkier and more expensive to purchase (or copy) than 'straight' guidance materials.

- It is too easy for students to skip the exercises.

Computer-based study skills development packages

There are many computer-based training packages aimed at developing various study skills, for example packages being developed at Napier University. These can be highly interactive learning materials, giving students good feedback on options that they choose, and offering them practice exercises which help them develop skills associated with learning from resource materials.

Advantages

- Many of these materials are enjoyable to work through, and students will find the time to use them well.

- These materials are necessarily interactive, and students can only progress through them by participating rather than just reading them.

Disadvantages

- Student 'throughput' is limited by the availability of the packages, the flexibility of the network system, and the number of machines on which students can access the materials. If a large group all need the same help at the same time, there are problems!

- Even when such packages provide a powerful learning experience, there is a tendency for that experience to fade once students leave the package. It's rarely possible for students to have their own copies of such packages, enabling them to return to them whenever they may need help.

Computer conferencing

Computer conferencing and e-mail are becoming much more common as a normal part of students' experience of higher education. Such media can be used to help students develop their skills, not only relating to electronic media, but also their skills in the use of other kinds of learning resources. Such an approach has already been used at Glamorgan University.

Advantages

- It is possible for individual students to get specific feedback to their questions and problems, both from tutors and from fellow students.

- Such media can be used at any time, and there is no need to plan the study skills support into allocated time-slots.

Disadvantages

- Student access to computer conferencing is often limited by the availability of networked terminals and the opening hours of resource centres.

- In some disciplines, it is difficult to get students (and staff!) over the hurdle of interacting with computer conferences.

Credit-rated study skills modules

In many institutions, including Glasgow Caledonian and Sunderland universities, there are now modules specifically devoted to study skills or learning strategies. It can be argued that this is a major step in the right direction, and that the most important outcome of higher education is that students should have become better at learning and making use of a wide range of learning resource formats.

Advantages

- Where such modules 'count' alongside subject-specific modules, students are given a clear message that developing their learning strategies is worth spending time on.

- The assessment when linked to such modules can engage students in learning from a variety of resource materials, and give them feedback on the strengths and weaknesses they demonstrate in such work.

Disadvantages

- Students can be dismissive about the value of such modules, and divert their time and energy to subject modules, perceiving the latter as 'more-real'.

- Such modules are time-intensive, and the availability of staff with the necessary skills and experience to run them successfully is very limited.

WHAT ABOUT ASSESSMENT OF THE RESULTS OF RESOURCE-BASED LEARNING?

There is a rising tide of dissatisfaction concerning the fact that assessment in higher education remains dominated by tutor-marked examinations and tutor-marked written coursework. The problems, and a proactive direction for solutions, have been captured by Brown and Knight (1994) and Brown *et al.* (1993); a range of contributions in Knight (1995) includes discussions of students' experiences of assessment. I've already alluded to the assessment of resource-based learning, but only insofar as mentioning the criteria against which learners' achievements should be measured. The criteria are important, but equally important are our answers to the following questions:

- Why do learners' achievements need to be assessed?
- How best may these achievements be assessed?
- Were the learning resource materials designed for *learning* or were they specifically designed to lead to assessment?
- What exactly should be assessed, to get the balance right between competence and values?
- Who is best placed to do the assessment? (For example, is some of the evidence relating to upholding values *only* assessable by learners themselves in practice?)
- Upon what basis should the assessment be scaled – if indeed it is appropriate to scale it at all?

> pass...fail?
> criteria fully met.................partly met.................not yet met?
> distinction..........................merit....................................pass?

- What *evidence* should be assessed? What kinds of evidence best lend themselves to assessment being valid and reliable?
- To what extent is the evidence a natural consequence of the resource-based learning being assessed, rather than an additional chore that students are required to produce for assessment purposes?
- To what extent may the success or failure of students depend on factors inherent in the learning resource materials, rather than on students' performance?
- How will the assessment associated with students' learning from the resource materials link with the other components of their assessment? Are students aware of the respective contributions to their overall assessment?
- How soon after using the learning resource materials will students' learning from them be assessed? Will assessment come too quickly for students to have properly digested what they have learned, or will assessment come too slowly, so that students may be depending on memory of what they learned?

INTERROGATING LEARNING RESOURCES

Ask of each learning resource:

- How does it increase learners' *wanting* to learn?
- What opportunities does it provide for practice, including trial and error?

- How can learners using it best get feedback on their progress?
- How well can it assist learners to make sense of what they're learning?

There are further important matters to consider. The following list of questions is worth reflecting on (and adding to) when appraising the choice of, or usage of, individual learning resource materials and media. For example, it is worth addressing each of these questions to the wide range of learning resource materials referred to in Ellington and Race (1993):

- How up-to-date is the material covered? How quickly will it date? Will it have an adequate shelf-life as a learning resource, and will the up-front costs of purchasing it or developing it be justified?

- How significant is the 'not invented here' syndrome? Can you work with the differences between the approach used in the material and your own approach? Can you integrate comfortably and seamlessly the two approaches with your students? If you criticize the learning resource materials your students are using, you're quite likely to destroy their confidence in using the material, and their belief in the quality of the content of the material as a whole.

- How expensive is the material? Can students realistically be expected to acquire their own copies of it? Can bulk discounts or shareware arrangements be made? If the material is computer-based, is it suitable for networking, and is this allowed within copyright arrangements?

- Where students can't have their own copies of a resource, are you going to be able to guarantee sufficient access to students? This is particularly crucial when large groups are involved. Could lack of access to essential resource materials be cited as grounds for appeal by students who may be unsuccessful when assessed on what is covered by the resource material?

- What alternative ways are there for students to learn the topic concerned? What complementary ways are there in which students can combine other ways of learning the topic with their learning from the resource material in question?

- How is the resource material or medium demonstrably better than the cheapest, or simplest way of learning the topic?

- Will it make students' learning more efficient? How will it save them time, or how will it focus their learning more constructively?

- Will the resource material or medium be equally useful to all students? Will there be no instances of disadvantaging of (for example) students learning in a second language, women students, mature students, students who aren't good with computers, and so on?

- What additional study skills outcomes will students derive from using the material? Are these outcomes assessed? Could they outweigh the *intended* learning outcomes?

- How can feedback on the effectiveness of the resource material be sought? What part should be played by peer feedback from colleagues, feedback from student questionnaires, observations of students' reactions to the material, and assessment of students' learning?

A TAXONOMY OF LEARNING RESOURCES?

Finally in this chapter, I would like to present a template for treating each of the various kinds of learning resources, to enable it to be analysed in a common format, exploring briefly its potential in the light of how students may learn from it, and how their learning may be assessed. This taxonomy, at least for now, is necessarily generic in nature, and you will almost certainly wish to interject conditional statements about each medium I attempt to analyse. This is perfectly healthy; the taxonomy I am going to present is just a starting point. Each question needs to be readdressed in the light of the circumstances of individual learning packages, individual types of learner, and the place the packages or media occupy in the context of the teaching and learning strategy adopted by each practitioner in their own field. To conclude this chapter, I will include some completed templates for selected types of learning resource material, ranging from the most basic paper-based ones to the more sophisticated technology-based ones. I will also include a blank template for you to pursue the same sort of analysis of the types of learning resource materials you may use in your teaching, in the hope that you find this a useful mechanism for reviewing their effectiveness in your context.

REFERENCES

Brown, S and Knight, P (1994) *Assessing Learners in Higher Education*, London: Kogan Page.

Brown, S, Gibbs, G and Rust, C (1993) *Strategies for Diversifying Assessment in Higher Education*, Oxford Centre for Staff Development.

Bourner, T and Race, P (1995) *How to Win as a Part-time Student* (2nd edn), London: Kogan Page.

Ellington, H I and Race, P (1993) *Producing Teaching Materials* (2nd edn), London: Kogan Page.

Knight, P (ed.) (1995) *Assessment for Learning in Higher Education*, London: Kogan Page.

Northedge, A (1990) *The Good Study Guide*, Buckingham: Open University Press.

Race, P (1992) *500 Tips for Students*, Oxford: Blackwell.

Race, P (1994) *The Open Learning Handbook* (2nd edn), London: Kogan Page.

Saunders, D (ed.) (1994) *The Complete Student Handbook*, Oxford: Blackwell.

HANDOUT MATERIALS

Ways in which they can promote...	Assessment considerations
Wanting to learn Saving tedious note taking. Presenting 'digests' of important information. Including information about learning targets and objectives.	*Nature of learning outcomes* Established principal areas that students should learn. Helping students to structure their learning of subject matter. Defining details of the syllabus and its assessment.
Learning by doing Can include activities and exercises for students to do during lectures and in their own time. Can refer students out to textbooks and other learning materials. Can suggest that students make summary notes during or after lectures, or after further reading. Can form a basis for discussing ideas with fellow viewers. Can be a basis for participating in group debates. Can be used by students for working out lists of questions of 'matters arising' from the handout.	*'Doing' that can be measured* Students' completion of exercises included in the handouts. Students' summaries made after studying handouts. Students' answers to set questions involving them doing further reading or research. Levels of participation in discussions of things covered in the handouts. The extent to which students apply critical thinking to the material in further tasks and exercises set after they have followed up the handouts.
Learning through feedback Handouts can include self-assessment feedback responses to exercises and questions. Handouts can include 'expert witness' feedback from tutors on important questions tried by students.	*Assessment and feedback* Tutors giving feedback about whether students have identified the most important features from the handouts. Giving live feedback on students' answers to questions arising from the handouts.
Making sense of what has been learned Handouts can include reflective reviews of different interpretations and approaches to a topic. Handouts help students to work out what are the most important factors on a topic. Handouts can help students by including annotated bibliographies and reviews.	*Suggestions about assessment criteria* Make sure that students know what they are expected to do with the activities and exercises in handouts. Make the criteria explicit so students know what they are expected to get out of the content of the handouts. Where possible, negotiate the criteria with students, so that they feel a sense of ownership of the assessment agenda.

COMPUTER CONFERENCING AND E-MAIL	
Ways in which they can promote...	**Assessment considerations**
Wanting to learn Can make notes available to students without them having to write them. Students can edit and personalize notes. Many (maybe most) students like playing with computers.	*Nature of learning outcomes* Helps develop students' communication skills. Helps develop keyboard skills. Can be a means of giving direct individual feedback to students on their marked work.
Learning by doing Can include activities and exercises for students to do with given textual material or other information. Can refer students out to textbooks and other learning materials. Can suggest ways that students are intended to add to the content provided to them. Can provide briefings regarding preparations students should do before attending lectures or tutorials. Can be used by students for working out lists of questions of 'matters arising' from the material.	*'Doing' that can be measured* Students' adaptation of the material provided. Students' work on exercises set using the medium. Students' answers to set questions involving them doing further reading or research. Levels of participation in discussions of things covered by the information supplied. The extent to which students apply critical thinking to the material in further tasks and exercises set after they have processed the information given.
Learning through feedback Tutors giving feedback about whether students have identified the most important features from the information supplied. Feedback can include 'expert witness' feedback from tutors on important issues raised by students.	*Assessment and feedback* Students can peer assess each other's contributions to conferences. Giving individual feedback to students on their answers to questions arising from the material.
Making sense of what has been learned Conferences can include reflective reviews (from students as well as from tutors) on different interpretations and approaches to a topic. The structure of computer conferences can help students to see the shape of a topic, and its place in the larger picture.	*Suggestions about assessment criteria* Make sure that students know what the participation expectations are for the conference. Make the criteria explicit so students know what they are expected to get out of the material on the system. Where possible, negotiate the criteria with students, so that they feel a sense of ownership of the assessment agenda.

VIDEOCASSETTE RECORDINGS	
Ways in which they can promote...	**Assessment considerations**
Wanting to learn Adding real-life dimensions. Seeing moving images. Colour and interest.	*Nature of learning outcomes* Sense of perspective on topic. Recognition of images. Analysis of real-world situations.
Learning by doing Preparing an agenda of what is being 　sought from the video. Making summary notes on or after 　viewing the material. Answering questions posed in workbook. Discussing ideas with fellow viewers. Participating in group debates. Working out lists of questions of 'matters 　arising' from the video.	*'Doing' that can be measured* Students' preparations to view a video. Students' digests made from watching 　the video. Students' answers to set questions. Levels of participation in discussions. The extent to which students apply 　critical thinking to the material.
Learning through feedback Gathering feedback from other students 　who have watched the video. Gaining 'expert witness' feedback from 　tutors. Feedback from other people about ideas 　arising from the video.	*Assessment and feedback* Giving feedback about whether 　students have identified the most 　important features from the video. Giving feedback on students' answers 　to questions arising from the video.
Making sense of what has been learned Putting theoretical ideas into a practical 　real-life perspective. Working out what the most important 　factors are on a topic.	*Suggestions about assessment criteria* Make sure that students know they are 　not just watching passively, but are 　going to be measured in some way. Make the criteria explicit so students 　know what they are expected to get 　out of watching the video. Where possible, negotiate the criteria 　with students, so that they feel a 　sense of ownership of the 　assessment agenda.

LEARNING RESOURCES TYPE	
Ways in which they can promote...	**Assessment considerations**
Wanting to learn	*Nature of learning outcomes*
Learning by doing	*'Doing' that can be measured*
Learning through feedback	*Assessment and feedback*
Making sense of what has been learned	*Suggestions about assessment criteria*

Chapter 4

Helping Individual Staff to Develop and Implement Resource-based Learning

Chris Rust and James Wisdom

Resource-based learning is currently being developed by staff in higher education who wish to implement new curriculum delivery methods for all the valid
reasons discussed in earlier chapters in this book. Too often, however, they are
thrown in at the deep end and are required to produce learning resources with
little help, guidance or money to do it. In some cases this results in the rehashing
of lecture notes into dull, dreary packages which lack any kind of student
interaction or visual interest.

This chapter, based on our experiences of working with staff who have been
moving towards resource-based learning in our own universities, addresses this
problem and suggests a seven-stage approach you can use to develop materials
covering:

- some clarification of reasons for using resource-based learning,

- an identification of the changes necessary to a programme of learning when
  introducing this method,

- some suggestions on how to undertake careful planning and preparation,

- a discussion of how teams can avoid reinventing the wheel,

- some guidelines on designing resource materials,

- a discussion of how the learning activities are to be incorporated, and

- a listing of some of the types of learning activities suitable for resource-based
  learning.

CLARIFICATION OF THE REASONS FOR USING RESOURCE-BASED LEARNING

If you are being asked to develop resource-based learning materials you need to
ask:

- What exactly is it you are hoping resource-based learning will achieve?
- What problems will it help you overcome?
- What developments will it aid?

Considering course evaluations and student feedback data, the subject librarian's annual course report, minutes of boards of study and course committee minutes can all provide you with clear indicators of the direction in which the course should develop. For example, if the student feedback is that the course is too heavily lecture-based and they would welcome some variety in the class sessions, you may need to produce resource materials which replace or supplement some of the content *and* provide class-based activities. On the other hand, departmental or subject librarians may have been reporting for some time desperate and unseemly squabbles in the library for the two copies of the text regarded as essential for a particular course of study. In this case, resource-based learning may lead you to assemble study-sets of articles and extracts, cleared for copyright and easily photocopiable.

In deciding on the form that the resource-based learning might take, you should constantly refer back to the purposes identified at the outset and question whether what is planned is the best method to achieve it. At each stage, the outcome should be checked against the rationale to ensure that the materials are fit for purpose.

IDENTIFICATION OF ALL THE CHANGES NECESSARY FOR A PROGRAMME OF LEARNING IF RESOURCE-BASED LEARNING IS TO BE INCORPORATED

Our experience shows that many staff start with very modest ambitions to introduce an element of resource-based learning and soon find themselves redesigning the whole of the undergraduate degree programme. It is also the case that very small changes in some course can have quite considerable knock-on effects and these must be anticipated and catered for. For example, in order to work well with the resource-based approach, students may need to be prepared through specific study skills guidance, as discussed in Phil Race's chapter. Similarly, if students are going to be required to work on materials independently in groups, provision will need to be made for spaces in which they can work, and they may also need training in group skills methods. It is also very likely that the assessment methods and media you use will need to be changed; even small packages of resource-based learning within a larger course may need to be separately assessed, as it may not be appropriate to try to incorporate such learning in an end of module exam. You then need to ask yourself about the nature and extent of the knock-on consequences of introducing resource-based learning on the course organization or structure overall.

CAREFUL PLANNING OF PREPARATION AND PRODUCTION OF RESOURCE-BASED LEARNING MATERIALS AND PROGRAMMES

Probably the biggest single issue to emerge from the identified changes will be the amount of time it will be necessary to allow, both to staff for the production and running of resource-based learning courses and for students in undertaking them. Before embarking on resource-based learning materials production, you need to question how they will find the necessary time to make the changes, and how the students' attendance and study time on the course are going to be affected.

For individual lecturers making changes to their own courses, a useful general guideline is to try to avoid doing too much too quickly. It is almost inevitable that inexperienced resource-based learning designers underestimate the time it will take them to do all the tasks associated with production. A planned programme of modest changes to a course over three years, with evaluations and feedback on these changes at each stage, is likely to achieve more than a heavy investment of time at the beginning without any follow-up, although there certainly will be a need for a great deal of work in the early stages. Such an approach also puts less at risk and avoids the potential for disasters. If one of your reasons for developing resource-based learning is to save staff time, and a start is made by specifically changing only one part of the learning programme in the first year, time saved in the second year can be reinvested into further developments.

For course teams, however, there can be economies of scale in making substantial changes in one go. Benefits can include: making best use of staff development sessions for groups of resource-based learning designers prior to starting a large-scale programme; cost-effectiveness in the production of materials; a more logical programme of student skills development; and more sensible use of teaching rooms and other resources which can be planned by teams rather than individuals. A further advantage is that any revalidation that is required to incorporate new teaching and learning strategies will only have to happen once.

With regard to the students, it is vital to identify as accurately as possible the time demands that proposed changes are likely to make on them. Experience shows that there is a tendency for staff to be carried away in preparing the most excellent and demanding course possible for potentially the most brilliant cohort of students they could imagine. This can then make quite unreasonable demands on lesser mortals. As a rule of thumb, the majority of universities in the UK indicate that students on a credit-rated programme are normally expected to study for about 1,200 hours a year. If a module or unit team is sharing the year's programme equally with up to nine other tutors, then your students may have as little as 120 hours to study your subject, which includes the time spent in lectures, tutorials, revision and assessment.

It is useful to focus on the ratio between students' time spent with tutors and their private study time; elegant and efficient resource-based learning stimulates the best use of the students' private study time without overloading them. In addition, most universities are keen to reduce the amount of class contact time between tutors and students, which can be achieved if resource-based learning materials are used within a mixed programme of study methods rather than, as often happens, being used in addition to the traditional delivery modes, causing excessive student workloads.

AVOIDING REINVENTING THE WHEEL

Before rushing into the preparation of your own new materials, you would do well to check whether there are appropriate materials already in existence for the purpose required. These may include complete packages available from other universities including the Open University or from commercial suppliers, materials that can be extracted and adapted under site licences; key reference books around which study materials can be developed; and other sources, including existing lecture notes, handouts and study materials for a course or unit that already exist within a department. Library specialists are well placed to advise you on what is commercially available as well as what is already used by other members of the department, unbeknown to you.

However, most lecturers are extremely reluctant to use materials which they themselves have not created. Their argument is often that their context is different and that the materials are not appropriate for what they want to do, and won't work with their own (highly specialized) students. This is frequently referred to as the 'not invented here' syndrome. The reason, however, is more likely to be bound up with our current conceptions about authority and its links with the ownership of knowledge. The problem is essentially an emotional one; as subject experts we do not want to give up the perceived expertise which seems to come from originating the materials ourselves. One of the skills which is needed for the successful design of resource-intensive courses is creative adaptation; to be able to see things from the students' viewpoint, and the ability to disaggregate, remodel and reassemble other people's carefully designed products for local use in different contexts. If greater use is to be made of resource-based learning, we need to accept that a transition is being made from subject experts as creators of knowledge to tutors as facilitators of student-centred learning. Once tutors can accept this change of parameters, it becomes easier for us to benefit from the ground work that others have put in.

For large and diverse first-year classes, for example, study guides can be developed based on one or two recommended key texts. These can be targeted at different cohorts of students so that the activities and examples are relevant to their own disciplines, and assessment activities can be varied according to the level at which students are studying. Depending on previous experience and ability, students can then be guided through different parts of the texts. Remedial loops can be provided for those who need it, and extended reading in other sources recommended for those for whom it is appropriate.

GUIDELINES ON DESIGNING RESOURCE MATERIALS

In designing good resource materials, you should consider the following.

What kind of structure the materials should have

Tutors need to decide on the way in which the elements of the resource-based learning materials will fit together, remembering that it does not necessarily have to be linear. It is possible to encourage students to move between sections in their own order or to construct alternative pathways. It is also vitally important that any sequencing fits comfortably with the students' processes of learning, allows time for consolidation, and pays particular attention to the timing of assessment.

How the material can be broken up into manageable chunks

In general, it is a good idea to make sure your material is divided into clear and manageable chunks. Each chunk should contain the following: precise learning outcomes, relating to an identified topic, question or hypothesis; a task or activity (see below) with some form of assessment which provides feedback to the student and possibly leads to further action; and a summary/review. It may also be useful to direct the students to other support materials outside the course materials.

How the material can be made personal to the reader

It is generally agreed that resource-based learning materials should be read as if the writer were speaking to the reader. Getting an appropriate voice for resource-based learning materials is a skill that often needs development, to avoid sounding over-patronizing or distant. Excessive use of impersonal forms can be really off-putting for students.

The most appropriate style of production to be used within the budget available

It is vitally important that any materials are attractive. Materials designers should keep asking the question: Would *you* want to use them? Students will need a clear introduction and overview, good sign-posting so they know what stage they have reached, a course 'map' showing the scope of the materials and the possible routes through it and, above all, the material must be easy to use (even if the subject itself is ferociously difficult).

In the case of written materials it is generally recommended to have large amounts of 'white space', with text broken up by illustrations and diagrams where possible and sufficient typographical and layout variations to avoid presenting dull pages full of words. If the student is expected to write answers into the materials themselves, the amount of space provided (perhaps in a box) will be a clear indication of what is expected. It is worth noting that if no written answer is required, the student may well not engage with the question. For example, simply having the question, 'To what extent do you agree with the views expressed in the extract you have just read?' may lead the student to a perfunctory mental grunt. The task, 'List those points with which you agree/disagree', together with the space in which to write them, is likely to be more productive. It is also a good idea to give time indications along with tasks. Race (1994) develops these issues further.

Two final considerations to be borne in mind in preparing materials are first, to avoid repetition by looking for variety in the overall student experience and the tasks and activities which they are offered, and second, to maintain consistency in the typography and the way that materials and tasks are presented, for example, the guidance/requirements might all be in italics, tasks in boxes and so on. The aim is to provide a sense of continuity without being boring.

The support mechanisms to be provided for students

Most resource-based learning involves an element of independent study and therefore you need to consider building in sufficient support mechanisms to ensure that the students are learning effectively. These may include:

- *Aids to study:* prior to any task, you should ensure the students have some guidelines and advice on the processes and skills they may need to use. For example, prior to a group task, the students may benefit from some guidance on group processes and on how best to organize themselves.

- *Overview and review lectures:* the purpose of these is not to provide lecture-specific content in depth but to take advantage of one of the best features of lecturing, namely the opportunity to provide reviews and summaries of material studied independently. They can also perform a social function in bringing the students together and maintaining a course identity, as well as providing an opportunity to deal with areas with which the students appear to be having problems.

- *Feedback opportunities:* through informal self-assessment, peer review and comment, or formal assessment at regular intervals, the students can be provided with feedback on their progress.

- *Remedial loops/surgeries:* for those students who appear to be having problems it may be possible to provide additional materials and/or offer 'surgeries' for them to attend.

- *Staging posts:* at certain points in the course, students may benefit from being able to review their progress. Some of these methods have already been mentioned (informal and formal assessments, and review lectures) and others might include reporting to a base group of other students or meeting in individual or group tutorials.

HOW THE LEARNING ACTIVITIES ARE TO BE INCORPORATED

The extent to which this is achieved effectively will be a principal determinant in the success (or otherwise) of the resource-based learning materials.

> Effective resource-based learning has more to do with designing appropriate learning activities than writing down course content. It is not so much the content itself as what students do to get to grips with it that matters: a relatively uninspiring textbook can be turned into resource-based learning material through the addition of imaginative activities. (Wisdom and Gibbs, 1994)

Before designing any specific activity, it is useful first to consider the following questions.

Would the activity be better as an individual or group task?

If individual tasks are chosen, would they nevertheless benefit from some form of collaboration, where this is possible, by students working in parallel, perhaps through the use of tutorless groups? Are there instances where that would be perceived as cheating or encouraging plagiarism? Sometimes students feel they should be competing with each other for the best marks or for positive recognition from staff (as both of these are thought to be in limited supply). It is possible to guide students' behaviour by clearly stating the ground rules for any assignment.

Where should it come in within the course?

It is probably desirable that the activities should be early in the course if they are to be diagnostic, and if use is to be made in some way of any outcomes. Activities can be used to help students plan their routes through the material, or to have a confidence-building function, by giving an opportunity for modest, early success with a relatively easy task.

If the activity is to offer the opportunity to apply theory to some practical problem, or to use an example to derive some underlying theory which relates to what has already been covered, it will be best placed in the middle of the course, once a basis of understanding has been established.

If, however, the activity is designed to integrate a number of earlier features, or to relate the material to other parts of the students' experience (such as to other courses or to their knowledge of any real-world practical application), or is to act as a summative evaluation of how much the student has learned from the course, then it will need to occur towards the end.

What skills are the tasks designed to develop?

These may be skills specific to the subject discipline – skills which might help the students learn in other sections of the course, or the more generic and transferable skills which all graduates should be developing, such as problem-solving and effective communication. Of course, these skills are not necessarily mutually exclusive, so a single task may satisfy a number of skills needs.

How substantial should the activities be?

It can be helpful to give guidance to students on how long any task should take, to avoid skimping by the low achievers and excessive time on-task by the over-zealous. However, it is important that these time estimates should not be just guesses. If you undertake the tasks yourself, this may give a rough guide, but it is far better to pilot the tasks with real students at the right level, so that expectations can be matched with students' actual performances.

How frequently should students encounter tasks within the resource-based learning materials?

Usually, students new to a subject or a process benefit from frequent feedback on small stages of learning; as they grow in confidence and understanding, students can respond to the challenge of handling larger quantities of information or more varied and complex tasks. However, it is rarely sensible to leave students reading or watching material for long stretches of time without prompting interaction.

What types of task have they already done?

It is a good idea to avoid repetition and to keep the process interesting, by varying the type, duration and extent of activities required. However, some kinds of activity provide great benefit from being consolidated through regular exercises which deepen or broaden the students' understanding.

To what extent is the activity about promoting interaction, or is it principally about assessing progress?

In many cases, activities in resource-based learning are written in the tone and language of assessment, even if they are only intended to be guidance. If the activity is mainly designed to get students to look for ways in which to integrate their learning with what they already know, perhaps in the workplace or in relation to other subjects studied, then framing the questions in ways that sound like assignments will be less than helpful. It is also really important that you provide the right kind of responses to questions to give feedback and encouragement, as discussed in Race (1994).

Will the task require some preparatory skills development or guidance?

Perhaps the students may have developed some skills or understanding from an earlier part of the course, to which a reminder reference might be made. It is vital to provide links between the sections of the material, as students may be experiencing long gaps between the times they have available for study. These links should be explicit, encouraging and informative, giving enough detail to remind students about elements of earlier study without being repetitive, rather than drawing attention to students' forgetfulness by suggesting they should be able instantly to recall earlier work.

TYPES OF ACTIVITIES

There are so many activities which can be included in resource-based learning it would be impossible to cover them all. The first set of activities described here can probably be best used by individuals but can also form the basis of group activities; the second set usually works best when used by pairs, threes or small groups.

Activities for individuals (or groups)

Responding to a checklist or questionnaire

These devices can be ways of summarizing previous sections of a course, focusing students onto the material which will feed into the work they are about to do. Of course, if students find they cannot respond to parts, it is a clue that they may wish to revisit earlier material!

Answering self-assessment questions

This sort of question is widespread in resource-based learning, but is sometimes not very effective. There is no way of being sure students have worked on them, and if they are offered the answers elsewhere in the package, it may be depressing to watch students flipping between the two pages without apparently tackling the questions.

Another common mistake is to write the questions using exactly the same language, even the same sentence structure, as was used to present the material in the first place, so the replies can be established from the text and the grammar rather than from understanding the material. Also, many of these questions have a common underlying question known as, 'Guess what the teacher is thinking', and students address themselves to that rather than to the material.

Finally, many students use the questions and answers as extra instruction rather than a test of their knowledge or understanding. Good, productive questioning requires imagination, cunning and empathy; it may be easier to set up useful problems that seem to be as difficult for you as for the student.

Providing exercises which can be done after reading a section of the materials

These include requirements to:

- redesign, reshape, edit material, perhaps for different audiences or readerships
- rewrite material in a different style to demonstrate understanding
- paraphrase, summarize or précis longer items
- critique or prepare counter-arguments for opinion pieces
- identify and mark key points under given headings
- prepare questions for discussion
- prepare questions for examination.

Applying the material to the context of the rest of the course

This involves finding the links and discovering the challenges and contradictions. It also covers applying the material to different contexts.

Designing (either really or in a simulated environment) an object, a system, a process, a technique

This can be done for real or in a simulated environment, using the new material learned within a resource-based learning package.

Applying the material to a case study or to a problem scenario

Writing an appropriate case study to make the most of the material; perhaps adding a further dimension to an existing case study.

Manipulating problems

Making calculations, attempting solutions, working out costings.

Relating personal experience to the material learned

Writing, then analysing, an appropriate critical incident; recalling best/worst experience and relating it to the material.

Using methods which concentrate on the process of learning

This includes keeping a diary, a learning log, reflections and commentaries.

Activities for use by pairs, threes or small groups

Discussion processes

> Open and free-ranging discussions
> Using checklists or questionnaires
> 'Read and tell' activities, reporting to a group on delegated different reading tasks
> Interviews, role plays
> Activities modelled on examination *viva voce*
> Debates, including balloon debates
> Adoption of contrary positions and using the roles of 'devil's advocate'
> Brainstorming
> Problem-solving processes
> Using peer support in the coordination of self-help groups
> Devising and managing a project based on the resource-based learning material.

Reporting processes

> Pooling results from investigations or other activities, leading to either group or individual reports
> Exchanging and commenting on drafts of assignments
> Providing written reports to tutors and to fellow students
> Giving oral reports to experts, to interested lay participants, to strangers with no previous knowledge.

CONCLUSIONS

There is often a great deal of goodwill among staff who are preparing to embark on the production of resource-based learning materials, which can easily be lost if they are starved of support and resources. The processes described here can help you to maintain momentum and enthusiasm, so that your commitment can be maintained and so that useful, interesting and user-friendly resource-based learning materials can be developed and used effectively by you and your students.

REFERENCES

Race, P (1994) *The Open Learning Handbook* (2nd edn), London: Kogan Page.
Wisdom, J and Gibbs, G (1994) *Course Design for Resource-based Learning in the Humanities*, Oxford Centre for Staff Development.

Chapter 5

Staff Development for Using Resource-based Learning

Sally Brown and Brenda Smith

Staff and educational developers have a key role in the successful implementation of resource-based learning. It is imperative that the individuals and teams who are developing and using the materials are supported effectively, so that the energy and commitment they invest are maximized. In many universities, this is undertaken very effectively but in others resource-based learning development is uncoordinated and anarchic. Much has been done by the HEFCE-funded 'Course design for resource-based learning', described in Chapter 2. Learning from this project and from the experiences of colleagues in universities in the UK and elsewhere, this chapter explores some of the areas in which staff may need help from staff and educational developers, and suggests ways in which this can be undertaken.

WHAT ARE THE REQUIREMENTS OF THOSE WISHING TO IMPLEMENT RESOURCE-BASED LEARNING?

We suggest that individuals and teams frequently need help in the following.

Changing their roles from information transmitters to facilitators

Resource-based learning places more emphasis on the materials than on the deliverer, and sometimes academic staff find it difficult to come to terms with this new role. When tuition is by traditional lectures, the content of the material is entirely within the control of the lecturer, who can adapt, insert, omit, update, emphasize and reframe material, on the spot, as they feel appropriate. They control the pace of the delivery and the nature of the student activity (as listener, largely).

With resource-based learning the material is written or edited by the tutor, but may be modified by a course team editor and may be offered widely on a range of courses for which it was not originally written. The way the material is used by students will be (literally) in the hands of the students who may skim, read in depth or ignore any areas they wish, working for short or long periods and in times and places of their own choosing. The role of the tutor in these circumstances is less as the omniscient one and more as just one of the resources available to students. Some staff may need support in learning how to be effective on these terms.

Helping them support learners

Merrison (1996) has described a number of negative factors associated with using learning resources, including isolation, lack of adequate feedback, problems with understanding the material, anxiety about ability, lack of motivation and lack of peer-group contact. Staff are sometimes anxious about how best to do this.

Changing their writing style

Academics are used to writing for publication and frequently do so very well. The language of the scholarly journal and the academic text is familiar to many who teach in universities and there is a great deal of expertise available in its production. However, resource-based learning materials work best when the language is simple, user-friendly and accessible, as the users who form the audience for them often work at a much less sophisticated level linguistically (Race, 1989). The text in workbooks and on screen needs to be broken into chunks which are readable and accessible. Visuals and layout are highly important for the MTV generation of students who are used to very high production values in different media and the writer needs to think about what the student is actually doing at all times, building in varied and appropriate activities.

Using new technology

Resource-based learning materials are being developed in a wide range of media, and many staff may feel uncomfortable about their skills in these areas. While they might feel relatively confident writing text to be used in paper-based packages, the idea of writing in Internet-usable mark-up language or of preparing video, text, graphics and sound can be quite terrifying. Fear of the technology can result in extremely cautious approaches by resource-based learning developers or can put them off making an attempt in the first place.

Working out the cost of course delivery using resource-based learning

Academics are unaccustomed to thinking about how much curriculum delivery methods cost, and sometimes make errors because they fail to take into account how much materials cost to develop, reproduce, update and deliver.

Preparing lectures is time-consuming but most lecturers have a reasonable idea of how long it is likely to take them and hence the approximate likely cost of curriculum design and delivery. This is much harder to estimate with resource-based learning and there are complex sums involved in establishing the cost-effectiveness of the various media. The main preliminary work in this area has been done within the HEFCE-funded resource-based learning project, led by Graham Gibbs (Gibbs *et al.*, 1994); he refers to this in Chapter 2.

Developing materials that are transferable to different contexts

When developing materials, particularly those which are costly, it is important to bear in mind the need for them to be suitable for different kinds of users. The expense of designing, developing and producing learning resources is rarely justifiable if they are usable in only very limited contexts, or for one-off occasions. Andrew Charlett (Chapter 7) and Nick Slope (Chapter 9) explore these issues further.

Making good use of materials written by others

Academic staff are often wary of using resource-based learning materials developed by others, because they find context-specific references off-putting. However, it is enormously wasteful of resources if effectively the same material is being written consecutively by individuals and teams, when collaboration and customization at the point of use could be more cost-effective. They need to identify what already exists in specific disciplines and selectively to use what is relevant to their own areas.

Making better use of resource centres

Often facilities exist in universities of which staff are unaware, or which are under-used because their location or hours of opening are unsuitable. It is important that dissemination of information is undertaken so that resources can be better used.

Working as a member of a team

Increasingly, curriculum delivery is not a task for 'lone heroes'. Resource-based learning tends to be a collaborative process with academics working alongside educational staff developers, technicians, administrators, librarians and other tutors. This may be a complex process for those who are used primarily to working on their own. Team-building activities and coordination are needed so that the skills of all stakeholders are used to best effect.

Guiding a team of distributed deliverers

Resource-based learning materials are frequently used by a variety of staff in different contexts and locations. The more people who are involved in course delivery, the more important it is that the team are briefed and updated effectively, so that they are all working on the same ideas. Teams using the same materials need to get to know each other, identify common problems and start to talk the same language.

Planning resource-based learning projects

Project management skills are necessary for the design and production of resource-based learning materials, particularly since deadlines and costings are usually tight. Teams often need help with the allocation of roles and the setting of time-lines to ensure achievement of goals. They need to be able to establish where they are starting from and what actions need to be taken, so they can plan effectively and evaluate what they have achieved.

SATISFYING DEVELOPMENT NEEDS

In the second part of this chapter, we offer a range of suggestions about how these identified needs can be satisfied. Obviously the amount of time and resources we can commit to this will vary from institution to institution and no single person or unit can expect to offer all we suggest below, but here we indicate some of the ways in which staff and educational developers could work with colleagues.

Raising awareness about the key resource-based learning issues at a number of levels

Help to write an institutional policy statement on resource-based learning aspects of teaching and learning.

Run seminars and workshops at both central university level and at departmental or module/unit.

Work with individuals who have identified needs.

Form networks of staff who are interested in resource-based learning.

Hold exhibitions of relevant materials, for example, those available from the Open University, Sunderland University and the Open Learning Foundation.

Broker visits to other institutions where resource-based learning is working well.

Encourage attendance and participation at relevant conferences.

Include material about resource-based learning in newsletters or in-house journals.

Put individuals in touch with others who are using resource-based learning.

Encourage collaboration with other universities at individual and departmental levels.

Compile a bibliography of available resource-based learning materials.

Influencing policy at senior management level

Write policy papers based on state-of-the-art knowledge and developments.

Organize high-profile events with external high-level experts.

Make presentations at senior management conferences.

Present papers at senior faculty and department boards.

Offer 'show and share' sessions, particularly for senior managers so they can see what can be done.

Provide costed proposals for realizable resource-based learning implementation.

Make use of the committee structure and target key individuals to champion resource-based learning.

Make use of the validation/review procedures and quality reviews to promote resource-based learning.

Helping staff to collect, analyse and adapt existing materials

Use our own contacts to help put them in touch with other users.

Provide collections of sample materials in our resource centres.

Run workshops to help them evaluate resource-based learning materials.

Advise them on copyright issues associated with adaptation and use of material produced by others.

Providing technical support

Raise awareness of what is available and what can be achieved with technology in support of resource-based learning.

Buy in expertise where the institution cannot provide it centrally to support developments.

Loan out our own experts to work alongside those wishing to develop materials.

Broker work-shadowing so staff can learn on the job by observing and working with those in their own institution who already are experts.

Disseminate relevant publications.

Support the use of students on placement, for example, from computing or information and library management courses.

Help cost out technical requirements and maintenance and replacement cycles for equipment.

Helping staff support learners

Help them to think about students' learning styles and how they are best suited to different kinds of students.

Advise them on the kind of support needed before programmes start, during the programme and after it has finished.

Put them in touch with others who are experienced in working with resource-based learning.

Promoting networking on the use of resource-based learning

Set up electronic conferences and e-mail/World Wide Web discussions to open debate and foster discussion.

Organize events attracting participants to form networks (for example, providing the seed corn in the form of a free lunch at a seminar).

Use staff development coordinators in departments to put staff in contact with users of resource-based learning and then link them up with each other.

Use teaching and learning newsletters to promote debate on issues of the design and use of resource-based learning.

Arrange teleconferencing/develop video-conferencing opportunities for staff at different locations to discuss resource-based learning usage.

Publish examples of good practice, for example, by the use of *Red Guides* at the University of Northumbria at Newcastle (see Chapter 12).

Link our staff into nationwide networks, eg, the Staff and Educational Development Association's flexible Learning in Higher Education network, the Universities and Colleges Staff Development Agency, the Open Learning Foundation, the Association of Learning Technology, the Educational Broadcasting Trust, the Teaching and Learning Technology Programme.

Use and set up regional groups, for example, the M1/M69 grouping of staff and educational developers in universities in the Midlands which runs a programme of activities and events for staff each semester.

Use international networks, for example, the International Consortium for Educational Development.

Helping staff to use bought-in experts

Make available lists of centres which can provide staff and educational development in resource-based learning.

Run conferences using external speakers and workshop leaders.

Recommend to potential resource-based learning users individual experts we know to have valuable expertise.

Advise on what published material is available on the Internet about resource-based learning.

Helping staff to use resource centres effectively

Offer support in the use of technological packages.

Provide review and preview material for trials.

Run demonstrations of packages and materials.

Provide facilities for staff to select and use materials available.

Buy in equipment for evaluation and piloting.

Arrange for demonstrations of equipment not currently available in the university.

Allow hands-on experience for individuals and groups.

Provide central facilities not available elsewhere.

Provide templates for material design.

Provide examples of really good resource-based learning material produced in the university.

Allow staff to experiment with materials in a risk-free environment.

Providing one-to-one support to staff developing resource-based learning

Read draft material and offer advice.

Suggest existing materials that could be considered for use and adaptation.

Provide advice and information about layout and presentation of resource-based learning materials.

Help staff to think about the variety of different media available.

Help staff to make materials more interactive by suggesting tasks to be interspersed with content.

Offer advice on different modes of assessment.

Offer advice on appropriate language, tone and register for resource-based learning material.

Help tutors to make a case for the use of resource-based learning at validation and review procedures.

Enable them to consider the student support requirements.

Offer them support in planning and managing the development of materials.

Help them evaluate the materials in use with students.

Support them in the maintenance and development of materials in use.

Helping resource-based learning designers to benefit from their work for their own professional development

Help them build evidence of their achievements to be used in NVQ portfolios.

Help them to disseminate good practice by writing about their experiences for publication and conferences.

Support their preparation of evidence for appraisal and performance review.

Encourage staff, particularly part-timers and those on temporary contracts, to use products of resource-based learning materials on cvs to demonstrate achievement.

Organizing and supporting institutional dissemination events

Run conferences at which best practice is described and demonstrated.

Organize open days in which staff can look at what is being developed in departments other than their own.

Facilitate poster displays and exhibitions at which staff can show how they are using resource-based learning in their area, with perhaps an annual award given for the most innovative and effective materials produced.

Arrange for demonstrations by aficionados.

Supporting team building events

Run exercises to help individuals recognize their own abilities and build their confidence to produce resource-based learning materials.

Organize team-building activities to help break down barriers and eliminate demarcation disputes, particularly when different categories of staff will be working together closely and equally for the first time.

Undertake SWOT analyses of the team to identify strengths, weaknesses, opportunities and threats in the implementation of resource-based learning.

Devise activities to help staff review each other's materials in a constructive climate.

Helping teams to consider values

Help them identify relevant equal opportunities issues and how these might affect material production.

Help them consider language and image so that it accurately reflects the potential user profile.

Encourage them to promote a reflective approach by learners.

Emphasize the need for student-centred activities.

Encourage them to build in a reflective approach, so they consider the process as well as the product.

Emphasize the need for quality audit, quality assurance and quality enhancement in the production and use of resource-based learning materials.

CONCLUSIONS

Inevitably, as staff and educational developers, our ability to promote the introduction of resource-based learning can only be effective where our activities are part of a team effort. Even so, we can act as change agents by making life as easy as possible for those who wish to move in this direction. Equally inevitably, the constraints under which we work, both organizational and financial, will affect the ways in which we operate, particularly in these current difficult times.

We recognize, therefore, that since fairly radical change in the ways in which students are taught in universities is inevitable (and exciting), we are well advised to use the full range of techniques at our disposal to support staff in implementing resource-based learning to the best of our ability, for the good of our institutions or academic colleagues and ourselves.

REFERENCES

Gibbs, G, Pollard, N and Farrell, J (1994) *Institutional Support for Resource-based Learning*, Oxford Centre for Staff Development.
(In the same series are nine subject-specific books looking at resource-based learning in Social Science, Education, Technology, Accountancy, Built Environment, Art and Design, Business, Humanities and Science, prepared by the project team.)
Merrison, B (1996) 'Supporting learners', *Open Learning Today*, Jan./Feb.
Race, P (1989) *The Open Learning Handbook*, London: Kogan Page.

Chapter 6

Implementing Computer-supported Resource-based Learning

Leslie Mapp

The Open Learning Foundation's remit is to assist in the development of new methods of teaching and learning. It has 26 UK universities amongst its members, each of which is encouraging wider access to higher education. Learning technology is an important component in these innovations, and the ideas expressed in this chapter arise partly from discussions within the Foundation's Learning Technologies Issues Group. The author is grateful for these colleagues' support. The author is also grateful to CTISS Publications for permission to include parts of an earlier article published in *Active Learning*, the CTISS journal.

INTRODUCTION

There is nothing new about public education using technology; almost every twentieth century invention has been used by teachers somewhere in an educational setting, and educational technology has become a respectable academic field in its own right. What is new about the 1980s and 1990s, however, is the widespread adoption of small computers (generically known as PCs). The first generation of these 'personal' desk-top computers arrived in the UK in the early 1980s and, since then, their extraordinary leaps in technical capability have been almost matched by the remarkable growth in their number appearing in UK institutions of education: a remarkable growth because throughout this time, which has seen millions of pounds invested in the technology itself, evaluation studies have reported equivocal results at best when seeking to register consequential improvements in learning. Even today, a decade and a half since the PC became widespread, and following continual experimentation and development, discussion still mainly centres on technology's *potential* rather than on replicable educational results.

Three arguments are often advanced for the lack of hard evidence concerning technology's effectiveness in education:

- that the situation closely parallels the wider relationship between computers and economic productivity, where a similar lack of evidence of clear benefit exists. This argument frequently cites the notion of 'critical mass' whereby an initial phase of unproductive investment is thought necessary to underpin later (ie, still in the future) benefit;

- that educational research has generally been methodologically flawed: using research tools from an earlier age to explain a qualitatively different new one. This argument also sometimes concludes that isolating the effects of computers from all other possible variables is in itself impossible, and therefore we cannot know their exact contribution;

- that education has been experimenting with immature technologies, themselves subject to development. This argument proposes that technology is only now reaching a mature enough stage to offer widespread educational benefit.

While each of these arguments may very well be true, it is the last argument which is compelling for anyone who has worked with educational technology since the arrival of the PC. The phenomenal growth in the PC's power and capabilities, and the silicon chip's use to develop allied technologies, has been explosive during the last 15 years. Several generations of computer-based educational technologies have passed (accompanied by several generations of educational technology experts). Simply staying up to date has been a considerable achievement.

Looked at historically, this wholesale adoption of immature technologies in education is not usual. The more common pattern is to wait until robust technical standards, pricing structures and dealer support systems are in place, that is, until a technology becomes a high street consumer item, before investing heavily, and then usually in previous-generation rather than cutting-edge versions. Thus, the overhead projector and the photocopier have become staple tools of education, as, recently, has the video camera, although its predecessor, the 8mm film camera did not, precisely because it remained a specialist tool, never reaching 'high street' status.

The unusually early adoption of computer technology by education has been made possible largely by government finance, frequently intended to encourage economic development. This general funding has virtually disappeared, replaced by smaller, targeted programmes such as the Joint Information Systems Committee (JISC) and the Teaching and Learning Technology Programme (TLTP). Institutions are now expected to meet almost all technology investment costs.

At the same time, however, computer technologies themselves are achieving levels of reliability and availability that make them worthy of consideration in their own right, not just as centrally funded educational experiments. The questions now become: is computer-based educational technology worth persevering with? Is our experience to date sufficient to base future decisions on? How should we build on existing, and implement new, systems to meet both educational and financial aims?

DEFINING SUCCESSFUL EDUCATIONAL TECHNOLOGIES

If we accept that the philosophy of higher education is moving from an emphasis on teaching to an emphasis on learning, we can define the most useful educational technologies as those which directly support learning. Of those technologies implemented to date, the most successful (which can often be identified by their ability to fit in and become invisible rather than those deemed the most glamorous) have been those supporting:

- improved information provision, eg, CD-ROM and on-line databases;
- complex simulations (including virtual reality), eg, science experiments; economic management models; three-dimensional visualization;
- distant communications, eg, electronic mail (e-mail) and computer conferencing.

(Also to be included in the list of successful educational technologies are those supporting academic networking, eg, JANET, but for these purposes we shall consider them to be indirect supporters of learning.)

Considering the application of these computer-based technologies to the 'traditional' practices of education, we can discern certain trends:

- lecturing is benefiting from audio-visual communication technologies, including videoconferencing;
- tutoring is benefiting from e-mail and computer conferencing;
- educational resources are benefiting from multimedia computing (including the Internet);
- students are benefiting from increased independence in the time, place and pace of their study.

Each of the individual technologies is being technically integrated within the so-called 'digital domain', the building block of the age, and in a manner that appears to be creating a viable industry in the same way that the invention of printing eventually resulted in the commercial publishing sector. If we assume that a viable industry is a prerequisite for long-term development (and early experience with educational software development run as a 'cottage industry' demonstrates this) we can put some confidence in the long-term viability of the digital information domain. The issue for educators, therefore, becomes one of how best to apply a range of technologies to improve learning.

In doing so, large questions are raised. If communications technology allows for distant education, what is the value of a campus? If simulations encourage group working, what will be a suitable method of assessment? If considerable investments are to be made in technology, how will they be justified in financial terms? And how will this be measured?

These questions demand careful answers. Infrastructures for printed learning materials in higher education are well established. The combination of commercial publishing companies, a pool of academic authors, and supporting library and reference facilities has formed a self-supporting whole. Eventually, if it is to survive, a similar infrastructure will develop in the digital domain, although it is quite likely to be a radical evolution of existing structures rather than a revolutionary change. In developing educationally effective applications of these technologies, a similar concern for creating systemic and sustainable initiatives must be seen. This requires that as well as tightly specifying technical systems, we must also tightly specify educational infrastructures if we are to succeed.

THE CONTEXT FOR IMPLEMENTING LEARNING TECHNOLOGIES

The single largest weakness in the application of educational technology has been the failure to adequately analyse user needs. Too-frequently reduced to hardware arguments, eg, Apple versus IBM, or screen design matters, eg, the location of icons, this area has been woefully inadequate in most cases. Successful implementation demands an holistic view, not one solely regarding the technology itself. Many people will have heard the anecdote about the first-time computer user who, on being asked to 'point the mouse at the screen', picks it up and points it like a TV remote control. It is an understandable mistake, using an existing skill to approach an apparently similar new task, but what is most revealing about this anecdote is that it is most frequently recounted to illustrate a *user* failure, which in my view is a clear case of blaming the victim.

Although called 'personal' computers, the effect of their large-scale adoption in education spreads much wider than the personal experience of students and staff, although these are not unimportant and are frequently underestimated factors. From experience to date, we can discern four elements which must be considered when thinking through an institution-led application of learning technology (that is, institution-led although the students and the learning may be widely dispersed):

- the institutional infrastructure
- the learning environment
- the quality of human and institutional relationships
- the effectiveness of the learning materials.

Many people in higher education have some experience within this framework but few have experience of (or still less influence over) the full range. Learning technology is more usually perceived from a partial perspective, by technologists, by administrators or by teachers. If learning technology is to become genuinely effective, and systemic rather than additional, it demands a more integrated approach.

Institutional infrastructure

This infrastructure creates the context for teaching and learning through policies and strategies, institutional aims and resource allocations. The most influential factors are:

- teaching and learning policy

- institutional strategic plans for responding to or creating educational and technological change

- policies on technical infrastructures – on common or diverse technical standards, on upgrading and on implementing new systems

- methods for resource allocation – including purchasing structures, and costing methodologies

- procedures for decision-making

- structures for maintenance and technical support

- policies on access, accommodation and security.

The clarity and effectiveness of these factors influence two important aspects of the implementation of learning technology.

First, long-term views on learning technology are necessary at institutional, faculty and departmental level because apparently simple decisions have long-term ramifications. For example, consider a requirement for students to produce word-processed assignments. It would benefit staff by making marking less arduous, and raises the possibility of electronic networking, increasing the potential numbers of students and enabling tutor support to be more direct and immediate via e-mail and conferencing. But will word-processors then be allowed in examinations? And if so, will spell checkers? If not, how will those students who are practised in writing on screen with author support programs, rehearse the skills of writing for examination without redrafts and grammar advisers? Indeed, will examinations still be the most appropriate form of assessment? These and similar consequential questions are raised by any technology innovation, and need answering before considering any particular computer package. A clear institutional policy on teaching and learning will frame much of this discussion; its absence will make the task harder.

Second, it is extremely important that informed management decisions are made. It is unfortunately true that in many institutions, managers have neither the time nor information to properly assess plans for implementing learning technology, yet find themselves both assailed by competing technical claims and academic visions, and expected to decide on some fine-line issues that even experts disagree on. There is a clear need for independent and expert advice to support management decisions. There is a similar clear need for considered educational objectives. Few cases of failure have been admitted in public, but almost all institutions report greater difficulties than anticipated and some level of disappointment in applying educational technology. Realistic assessments of educational evaluation results will help avoid unrealistic aims.

Managers at all levels need to be clear about the institutional context before considering any technology questions. In seeking to balance individual desires against institutional requirements (for example, a request for a particular word-processing package versus an institutional policy to purchase and support a different package), or to balance estimated income-generation for a new distance learning course against the true technology investment costs, managers need the assistance of explicit policies and clear procedures.

The learning environment

The learning environment involves all those factors necessary to promote effective teaching and learning, including:

- teaching and learning methods (eg, traditional, open learning, resource-based learning, self-managed learning, etc)

- access to resources by students and staff (including location)

- accommodation and facilities design

- the minimum necessary skills requirements of students and staff

- the availability of day-to-day educational and technical support, and of crisis support facilities.

Four of these factors are particularly important. First, the choice (or mix) of teaching and learning methods. Computer-based learning materials are most frequently specified to support some form of resource-based learning, with the intention that at least some part of the traditional teaching load should be borne by computers. However, research has shown that such technologies are not particularly good at direct teaching, except where the content can be conveniently sequenced and closely specified. It is no accident, for example, that the most successful uses of stand-alone learning technology are reported from the military or from banks and building societies, where common, repeatable processes are to be learnt by staff. Just as a good teacher or institution will employ a range of methods in response to differing educational needs, computer-based technologies need to be seen as *part* of the learning process, to be integrated with existing methods, augmenting them, rather than replacing them.

Second, the issue of the physical environment. In creating a learning environment simple questions of architecture are important. Architects understand the effect of built environment: people will behave differently in different places. The design of working spaces can encourage or discourage use, as will the hours of availability.

Third, the question of access and support. With communications technology having created 'virtual' communities among academics on JANET and the

Internet, their extension to student populations is a logical next step.

E-mail, conferencing and local cable television channels will extend and blur the boundaries between institutions and their students, but they demand new skills and new conventions. For example, there are acceptable times to telephone a professional builder at home, and some banks now offer 24-hour telephone services: what conventions will become acceptable behaviour among university teachers and students on a 24-hour communications network? And what services will such a university education require: 24-hour libraries; 24-hour technicians?

Fourth, the issue of skills. No advantage can be taken of any innovation if users remain inadequately trained. Technology should be transparent in use: the best contemporary example is arguably the telephone; a frequently cited bad example is the programmable video recorder – yet system crashes are a common feature of all computers. Technical skills are required for all computer-based applications, and both students and staff need to feel confident of their abilities. Equally important, however, is that users should be trained in techniques. These are not always difficult to learn and often experience teaches them, but they do need explicit consideration. For example, chairing a tutorial group by audio or video conference requires different interactions than a face-to-face meeting; it is not the same as leading a group in a tutorial room. Both students and staff need first-line training in order to maximize their effectiveness.

Relationships

The computer industry's notion of 'human factors' is more about behaviourist cues than human interaction in the way that, for example, cognitive psychologists or stress counsellors would understand the term. This reductionism has contributed to the generally poor design of both computers and their implementation. Although harder to define than technical or structural issues, the quality of human relationships is reported consistently by anecdote and by research as strongly influencing the quality of both an institution and an individual's experience within it. The human dimensions of innovation need to be included when considering the implementation of learning technology. Factors include:

- the general quality of working relationships: are they based on mutual respect? Are 'good days' achievable by most people most of the time?

- expectations: is the innovation matched to expectations, eg, will a new system meet staff aims to save time? Will an institution's expectation of increased efficiency be realized?

- project management: is sufficient information about changes available? And are all contributors to success being acknowledged? Are targets realistic and achievable? Are the responsible people able and willing to take decisions and make progress?

- individuals' responses: do people feel threatened or supported by the innovation? Eg, is this an attempt to replace jobs or to enhance teaching and
learning?

- the driving-force for change: is the impetus for innovation coming from the
'top down' or the 'bottom up'? And, whichever, do people feel sufficiently
involved in decision-making and sufficiently able to influence the results?

- resources: have sufficient resources, including time, been allocated to effect
the change? Is there enough training and day-to-day support?

- alternatives: are known, reliable systems being kept available while the new
system proves itself? Is there a review mechanism whereby modifications can
be made to the new system in the light of experience?

- plans for longer-term sustainability: is this change a group effort, or is success
dependent on certain charismatic individuals? Whichever, how are changes
to be secured?

Teaching and learning are intensely personal activities. Indeed, the changing
nature of relationships between staff and students is one of the most frequently
expressed consequences of the current changes in higher education and is
commonly reported as worsening. The demise of the personal tutorial is often
spoken of with regret, but the change is not just the result of structural changes
in HE: student expectations have also changed with the broadening of access
and the consequent diversity of student backgrounds. At the same time, structural changes are having their effect. Whether it be new teaching and learning
methods changing the role of university teachers from authorities to facilitators,
or growing numbers resulting in both institutional crowding and personal
isolation for students themselves, the nature and quality of human relationships
in higher education are changing.

Introduce technology and these relationships change again. There are reported cases of students resisting learning technology because they came to
university expecting to be 'taught'. However well-designed a teaching programme may be, it cannot succeed if students do not accept it; psychological
comfort is a known prerequisite of learning. Equally, if staff do not feel benefit
from developing new skills and techniques, they are less likely to implement new
approaches successfully, if at all.

Learning technology creates a triangular relationship between teacher, student and technology which replaces the traditional dual relationship between
tutor and student. This is a difficult enough change to implement successfully,
but in the current context where the arguments for adopting learning technology may be a conflation of the educationally sound and the financially expedient,
creating the institutional ethos, staff support and quality of student experience
which results in confident and skilled people is just as important to implementing learning technology as is choosing the right equipment.

Learning materials

The goal is educational effectiveness, which has been the subject of much educational research. This has resulted in a number of classifications systems for educational software, each of which tends to suggest that the important factors when considering learning materials are:

- having clearly defined learning outcomes: anticipated outcomes are usually devised prior to software evaluation, actual outcomes result from use

- the type of software involved, eg, whether it is intended to replace teaching, or offer remedial help, or provide a basic tool to support other activities such as research

- the demands on student and staff organization, eg to provide individual access or to assess groupwork

- the learning style(s) it supports, eg, convergent, divergent, deep, superficial

- the curriculum fit, eg, topic coverage, time taken to complete tasks

- the minimum new skills it requires to be used: its 'usability'

- the relation of software to supporting material (for study or as instructions)

- the system requirements, including demands for maintenance and updating.

Recent analyses of the benefits of computing technologies propose that while they have been effective in automating repetition, considerably expanding our ability to handle process tasks which can be expressed as numbers, they have been conspicuously unsuccessful in assisting with thinking and mental tasks. This would appear to be borne out by recent educational experience. In general terms, *information* has successfully translated to technology, witnessed by most university libraries with CD-ROM resources and on-line databases; and it is also clear that *communications* are migrating very successfully to technological forms. As yet however, *teaching* and *learning* have not been translated particularly effectively into technology, and *personal creativity*, while ably supported by word-processors, spreadsheets and paint programs, is not noticeably on the increase.

Much discussion of learning technology has centred upon the design of learning materials. The role and definition of interactivity, the specification of content; the place of moving video and audio; the differences between hypertext presentation and narrative – each has attracted considerable research effort, as has the evaluation of computer-based techniques among the repertoire of learning materials. Enough has been learnt to restrict early ambitions to replace other resources (including teachers) with computer materials, to the more realistic aim of augmenting the education process. It is generally true, however, that reliable examples of computer-based materials contributing significantly to improvements in learning are difficult to find.

A common defence for the generally poor performance of learning materials has been that 'little is known about how people learn'. In absolute terms this may be arguable, but the application of social and cognitive psychology to both medicine and marketing demonstrates how much more is understood about learning than commonly appears in technology-based learning material. Few programs do more than assume a model of student learning or allow for even the simplest differentiation between learning styles.

Although some assessment programs are 'adaptive', varying the pace and difficulty of questions according to the profile of previous answers, very few programs consider how to present information in different ways for different students. Designers tend to set out, particularly in hypertext/media applications, to enable students to find their own way around a program. In doing so, they run the risk of creating material in which content is atomized into free-standing, unrelated pieces; where concepts are not related in necessary sequences; and where the overall coherence of a subject is lost. What results may, from a designer's viewpoint, contain a comprehensive overview of the subject, but for a student may result in fragmented and incomplete learning (and research studies have shown that learning this way may also be slower).

THE FINAL STAGE

All of the above factors are influential on learning; their exact equation will determine the effectiveness of any new initiative. Where technology is involved, however, there is one further stage: specifying a system. In outline, there are ten elements to identify during this process:

- the compatibility of the new system with the existing technical context (if required)

- the anticipated number of users and the anticipated benefits to them – ie, the system's function

- the exact hardware required – everything, including cables and wiring

- the exact software required – everything, both system and user software

- the alternative systems available – and why they are not being specified

- the relevant suppliers, their prices and back-up facilities (including the stability of the company)

- the requirements for technical maintenance (both in-house and by special-ists)

- the support requirements, eg, for technical knowledge, for user training, for support, for upgrades, for supplying users with disks, for photocopying, etc

- the likely technical future, eg, how likely it is that this technology will be available in five years' time

- the full cost profile – at purchase, in year three and in year five.

These elements will create a *system specification*. Unfortunately, this is frequently skimped in real projects. Time spent on adequately specifying a system is never wasted; it is part of the learning process which helps establish the purpose and performance of a new initiative. Too little time spent on specification will result in an inadequate system, failed ambitions and frustrated expectations, all of which will undermine the proper implementation of technology-assisted learning.

However, system specification is not a simple job, and is usually too important to leave solely to technical staff. Their intention is to maximize the amount of computing power available, and to be seen by their peers as using the latest, greatest technology (as defined by the technical community rather than by educators). This is understandable, and their knowledge and enthusiasm is a vital part of the mix. However, the system's *function* is educational, and success should be measured in learning outcomes, not in megabytes. Consider the case of many institutions, whose expensive, inter-campus networks support inexperienced typists (students) in laboriously word-processing their essays, often during unsocial hours. This recreation of the Victorian classroom, with rows of PCs dedicated to overcoming poor handwriting, is hardly an estimable educational outcome.

System specification is a team effort. Technical staff and educators should work together, constantly checking their ideas with users or their representatives, including a reasonable cross-section of likely users: inexperienced as well as expert; women as well as men; part-time as well as full-time.

In the best implementations, the technology will become invisible, a tool with which to perform tasks or to think. A system boasting the highest technical specifications is a failure if it does not fulfil its role to be useful. 'I'm sorry the system is down', may not be heard as often as five years ago, but it is still far too frequent.

IN CONCLUSION

Implementing learning technology is a *cultural* activity, too often reduced merely to the technical. I have outlined the factors which most frequently influence the success of any initiative, factors which are evenly split between technical concerns and context concerns. Evaluation studies show that educationally successful systems are not necessarily the most technically advanced: success lies in the balancing of the technical, the educational, the institutional and the personal. If there is a single most influential factor however, it appears to lie in the clear definition of educational aims, of anticipated learning outcomes, together with a clear-eyed appraisal of possible technologies for their actual benefits, not for their image. While the future of education may indeed rest heavily on the implementation of technology-based systems, this is not the same as saying that education's future rests on the *latest* technologies. Education's future rests on good quality teaching and learning, supported by technology, be it the overhead projector, the photocopier and the video recorder; the telephone, the fax and the video conference; broadcasting, narrow casting, cable and satellite; or the computer, multimedia and the Internet.

The aim of late twentieth century higher education is multidimensional – to enable students to know (and continually learn about) their subject, to develop good communication skills, to develop an ability to learn independently, to develop good social and teamworking skills, and to develop an ability to adapt to changing circumstances. Computers alone will not do these things, but the combined strengths of institutions, teachers and technological resources might. It is technology *in context* that we should be looking for. I have tried here to outline this context.

FURTHER READING

Bates, A W (1995) *Technology, Open Learning and Distance Education,* London: Routledge.

Landeur, T (1966) *The Trouble with Computers,* Harvard, Mass: MIT Press.

Laurillard, D (1933) *Rethinking University Teaching – A framework for the effective use of educational technology,* London: Routledge.

Chapter 7

Networking with Associated Providers Locally and Nationally: A Case Study

Andrew J Charlett

BACKGROUND

At The Nottingham Trent University, a need was identified to provide an opportunity for students with a good HNC in Building Studies to obtain further qualifications, such as an honours degree in building by part-time study. This chapter describes the way in which a course has been designed and run at Nottingham Trent University which can offer a degree route through a franchise arrangement with a number of partner colleges, with students using a mixture of resource-based learning materials and face-to-face tuition.

In order to determine the needs of this group of potential students, a preliminary market research exercise was undertaken amongst existing and past HNC students in the East Midlands region. The results provided a profile of a typical student from this group. They were:

- Mature students (mid-20s to mid-30s) who had already completed a well–respected higher technician qualification or had obtained a significant amount of prior experiential learning within the construction industry.

- Potential students in jobs having a significant amount of responsibility, frequently at junior management level, involving management of the construction process. Thus their employers were often reluctant to allow them to pursue a conventional day-release course, since they could not spare them from these essential duties.

- People who were aware of their own professional integrity and commitment which restrained them from being absent from work frequently to undertake further study. This was often because they were concerned about what problems could arise within their area of responsibility while they were absent from work. They were also aware that if they took a 'day off' to pursue a conventional day-release course they would have to fi. five days' work into four when they returned to work.

- Students interested in taking control of their own study requirement having enjoyed a limited autonomy of study in their previous course.

In addition to this, it was recognized that the construction industry itself was going through particularly stringent cutbacks, due to the recession, and that this was having an impact on training budgets for staff wishing to enhance their personal development through the acquisition of further qualifications. From an analysis of this information, it was evident that an honours degree course in building by part-time study should be developed, utilizing resource-based learning materials, delivered by distance learning as described in Brown and Gibbs (1994), which would offer:

- flexibility of study, enabling students to study when they wished (frequently in their own time), where they wished (frequently at home) and how they wished (using a variety of learning mechanisms);

- choice of learning environment, enabling students to study where they felt most comfortable. This may be at home rather than in a conventional academic environment, such as a classroom;

- control over pace of progression, enabling students to study at the pace which best suited their acquisition of knowledge;

- empathy with career demands, enabling students to adjust their pace of study and progression with the demands of their career commitments. It may be necessary to take a break from study when work commitments are particularly onerous and to return to study when the work load is lightened.

However, it was also identified that there were some disadvantages with the full distance learning mode of delivery, such as:

- problems of isolation. Students may commence with tremendous enthusiasm, but this can wane as they begin to question whether they are putting the appropriate amount of effort into their studies or whether they are going in the right direction or veering off at a tangent;

- the need for regular reassurance from tutors regarding progress. Tutor support is not easily given from a distance. Students may wish to discuss their progress with a tutor face-to-face;

- the need to assess performance using other students as a benchmark. Students often set themselves targets of attainment based on their assessed performance compared to other students in the group. This bench-marking is difficult to achieve if other students studying the same course are unknown.

In an attempt to overcome these disadvantages, but still retain the important advantages of distance learning, it was decided to develop a hybrid mode of delivery which was entitled 'partial distance learning'. This meant that the course would be undertaken using resource-based learning materials in a distance learning format, but the learning process would be complemented by periodic visits to the university (Brown and Gibbs, 1994). These visits would provide the opportunity for:

- students to meet tutors and discuss their progress. This would enable students to focus on areas of concern to them, such as time for study or difficulties with the study materials. It would also enable tutors to highlight areas of concern they may have regarding the student's performance or time management;

- a programme of tutorials related to the material studied by distance learning to be undertaken. This would aid the learning assimilation process by focusing on issues highlighted in the learning materials and enable students to debate these issues with each other and with the specific subject tutor;

- the use of conventional learning, through workshops, for subjects such as IT where this mode of learning was found to be more beneficial. Students would have the opportunity to work with software packages under the expert guidance of a tutor who could assist them if difficulties were encountered;

- students to meet others pursuing the same course. This has a number of advantages. It enables students to compare their performance on the course with their counterparts. It also enables students to debate issues related to the distance learning materials in the seminars with other students from different backgrounds and possibly holding different viewpoints. Further, it offers the opportunity for students on the course to form self-help groups, which are regarded as useful support mechanisms for students engaged in distance learning (Nortledge, 1990). The organization of these self-help groups is left to the students themselves; they become more prevalent in the later stages of the course, where attendance at the university or college is less frequent.

The partial distance learning mode of delivery addressed most of the academic issues related to the course but created a further drawback, in that only students who could attend the university for the tutorial support could undertake the course. This limited access to the course and also its geographical area of operation. For the course to become viable, it needed to be networked to a number of associated providers situated around the country, each with a catchment area of approximately 5,000 square miles.

Many colleges of further and higher education have been eager to obtain an opportunity to offer degree programmes which have been developed and successfully operated by existing providers. The notion of franchising such courses to these colleges is particularly attractive to many of these providers and accorded with the aims of increasing access to this particular course. In consequence, a number of franchise agreements have been entered into, and their implications for the development and delivery of the course are the focus of this chapter.

EXPANDING DELIVERY THROUGH FRANCHISING

Franchising of further and higher education courses from established providers to new providers has benefits to both the franchiser and franchisees:

- franchisees are able to offer a degree course with an established pedigree. This becomes an extremely attractive opportunity for prospective students in their catchment area;

- the franchiser can expand delivery of the course to other parts of the country. This overcomes the problems of student access to a provider of the partial distance learning course;

- franchisees can obtain staff development through delivery of courses at degree level. This enables the college to increase its ability to deliver courses in the higher education sector;

- the franchiser is able to obtain revenue which can be used to further develop the course. Fees are charged on a per capita basis and adjusted each year in line with the retail price index. Revenue obtained is then used to administer the course, operate the quality assurance mechanisms and pay for the development and enhancement of resource-based learning materials used on the course;

- the collaborative arrangement established by the franchise agreement enables greater input to the development and delivery of the course from an enhanced course team. The subject tutors from each of the network providers have a stake in the ownership and delivery of the course. They are therefore eager to contribute to its development. This is achieved through the production of assignment exercises, examination questions and resource-based learning materials.

In order to ensure that the perceived aims of the course were being met by the franchise arrangement, two initial criteria needed to be satisfied by the prospective franchisee institution. First, the institution had to be capable of offering tuition and support to the standard established by the primary provider. This was assessed by consideration of the quality and level of courses already being offered within the institution and the qualifications and expertise of the staff who were likely to be involved in operating the course. Second, the institution had to be geographically placed so as to provide increased access to the course. In order to be able to offer a realistic catchment area to enable the franchisee institution a satisfactory opportunity to recruit viable numbers of students onto the course, it was essential that the institutions were sufficiently widespread not to be in competition with each other.

Thus it was possible to use the resource-based learning materials developed by the initial provider and supplement these with a programme of tutorials and workshops undertaken, at periodic intervals, by the course teams of both initial and networked providers as described in Brown and Gibbs (1994). The programme of tutorials and workshops was defined concerning topics to be considered, but not concerning content. This provided some flexibility and autonomy in delivery of the course by the franchisee institution, but did not affect the academic standard of the course, which is defined by the resource-based learning materials, course work assignments and examination questions, all of which are common. The same course is offered by all providers, but each provider adds their own distinctive flavour to its delivery.

Thus the subject tutors in each institution have the opportunity to discuss the issues raised in the distance learning texts with students in the seminar sessions, from their own perspectives. An agenda of topics for discussion in the seminar sessions is proposed by the university, but no structure as to how these discussions should be conducted is imposed. This flexibility in the delivery of the course is welcomed by staff in the franchisee institutions.

QUALITY ASSURANCE THROUGH COLLABORATION

The main critics of the concept of franchising in higher education have cited the erosion of quality standards as their primary cause for concern (Doyle and Russell, 1993). It has been claimed that higher education institutions are opting to franchise their courses as a means of obtaining extra revenue, without considering the possible consequences for the quality of the output being achieved by the franchisee institutions. This concern about erosion of quality standards is vitally important if courses are to retain their validity. It is therefore imperative that a great deal of thought must be given to quality assurance procedures before a franchise agreement is entered into.

Quality assurance procedures exist at two levels: the institutional and the course. The institutional level concentrates on the monitoring and control of quality through course committees, examination boards, faculty boards and finally the academic board of each institution concerned, and are well documented as standard formats. Quality assurance procedures at course level are less well documented as standard formats and it is these which need careful consideration if high quality standards are to be maintained. This involves monitoring the quality of learning being provided within lectures, tutorials and seminars as well as evaluating the standards of assessment provided by assignments, projects and examinations.

These procedures need to be complemented by reviewing feedback obtained from the learners themselves. On conventional courses, assessment procedures and feedback comments are often stringently evaluated, but frequently little is done regarding evaluating the quality of learning provision offered through the programme of lectures, tutorials and seminars. Thus the franchiser has little control over the provision of the learning experience on a conventional course operated within a franchisee institution, apart from providing the course syllabus to that institution and monitoring the assessment outcomes.

The adoption of distance learning as the study mode utilizing resource-based learning materials, provides considerable benefit in the establishment of quality assurance procedures at course level (Charlett, 1995). To begin with, the study material is common and has already been produced and tested by the franchiser. The study programme developed for use on the partial distance learning course by the franchiser can also be adopted by the franchisees. This includes common coursework exercises, examination papers, reading lists and study guides. This does not mean, however, that the franchisee institutions are mere tutorial outposts for the franchiser, with no significant input to the course. For franchising to work effectively it must involve collaboration between the participating institutions (Charlett, 1995).

Collaboration encompasses input to all the components provided by subject tutors at the franchisee institutions and monitored by subject leaders at the franchiser institution. This involvement is a gradual process and only comes about after the franchisee institutions have been operating the course long enough for members of their course team to feel confident that they can make a substantive input to the course. They are assisted in this endeavour by a number of staff development events and the formation of a network of lecturers with common interests associated with the course.

Such staff development events for the course described here are organized on a regular basis (normally once a year) by the franchiser. The topics are mutually agreed between the partner institutions and have included advice on operating and administering the course, preparation of distance learning materials, supervision of dissertations, assessment and marking of dissertations, operation of courses at honours level, accreditation by professional institutions, marketing of the course and research strategies.

By far the most important benefit of this collaboration, however, must be the contribution made by members of all the course teams involved to the planning and future development of the course. This involves forums of course leaders and common interest groups, comprising subject tutors and support staff. The expedience in this is that the course benefits from the collective wisdom of an enhanced course team.

Each franchisee institution organizes its own course board once per term, in which issues relating to the operation of the course within that institution are debated. The course coordinator from the franchiser is a member of each of these boards and uses these meetings as an opportunity to visit each institution in turn as part of the overall quality assurance procedures.

In addition, the franchiser holds a course management meeting once per term, in which issues relating to the overall development and management of the course are considered by the course leaders from each institution operating the course and the agenda for the main course committee is set. The course committee meetings are also held once per term and are the forum in which decisions are made regarding the management and development of the course. Each franchisee institution is represented (generally by the course leader) at this meeting.

An examination board meets once per semester to consider examination papers for each examined module on the course. This also comprises representatives from each participating institution, plus the external examiners.

At the end of the academic year the external examiners, together with the course coordinator, visit each franchisee institution, in turn, to examine assessed assignment and project work, together with marked examination scripts and, following the completion of this, make results recommendations at an examination board meeting in the institution. These visits culminate in the main examination board, held at the franchiser institution, in which the results recommendations from each franchisee examination board are discussed and ratified.

Of course this does not come without a price. The task of coordinating the effective delivery of a course of this type through eight institutions (with more waiting to join) is massive, and has involved the employment at Nottingham Trent University of an administrator whose job it is to ensure that arrangements for the delivery and assessment of the course are adhered to by all concerned. The job of overall course leader is extended by the requirements of coordinating the operation of the course within each franchise institution. This entails a substantial amount of travelling around the country to attend course boards and examination boards and to ensure that the quality assurance arrangements established by the franchiser are maintained.

As for the franchisee institutions themselves and their perceptions of the process, although they were extremely keen to become part of the scheme, it has taken a considerable amount of time and effort to establish a system where they feel that they are collaborating partners, rather than merely tutorial outposts of the university. This feeling of collaborative partnership has been engendered through a democratic process of consultation and involvement in the administration and development of the course through the formal structure of course board, course committee and course management meetings and the informal process of constructive discussion brought about by the formation of subject interest groups, involving tutors from each of the participating institutions. The partnership is now so strong that the more established franchisee institutions are offering help and support to those institutions which have only recently joined the scheme.

CONCLUSION

The development of a distance learning course involves the allocation of a substantial amount of resources, not least of which are the commitment and enthusiasm of a dedicated group of staff who are prepared to develop the distance learning materials and provide the ancillary support necessary to ensure that the course can be delivered effectively and to the quality standards expected. However, as work and study patterns change, so we are witnessing a steady move away from the constrained nature of conventional day-release courses towards the more flexible approach offered by distance learning.

It is also apparent that many students embarking on distance learning courses require a considerable amount of supplementary support. The model of the partial distance learning course may provide a solution to this dilemma, but lacks the universal accessibility of conventional distance learning, without an established network of centres which can offer the supplementary support required.

Collaboration with other suitable institutions, through franchising, offers this increased accessibility, together with the substantial opportunities for higher level work by the franchisee institutions and the benefits of extra revenue for further course development and an enhanced course team to assist in that development, on the part of the franchiser. This collaboration, however, must not be done at the expense of a reduction in quality. Thus, strict controls over quality mechanisms must be enforced. If this can be effectively achieved, then collaboration must be seen as being beneficial, not prejudicial, to future course development.

REFERENCES

Brown, S and Gibbs, G (1994) 'Using RBL to support learning on part-time courses with minimal attendance', in *Course Design for Resource-based Learning: Built environment*, Oxford Centre for Staff Development.

Charlett, A J (1995) 'Assessing quality with collaboration in delivery of courses through franchising', in *Developments in Education and Training Force Professionals in the Built Environment: Quality through inter-professionalism and collaboration*, University of Central England.

Doyle, N and Russell, L (1993) 'Franchised degrees come under attack', *New Builder*, 180, 25 June.

Nortledge, A (1990) *The Good Study Guide*, Milton Keynes: The Open University.

Chapter 8

Setting up Open Learning Resource Centres in Organizations: Learning from Experience in Industry

Amanda Scott

INTRODUCTION

Organizations of all kinds and sizes are moving towards setting up facilities where staff can undertake personal development and training, working at their own pace in accessible locations. This chapter gives an overview of some of the main issues for consideration, based on the experience of the work of Pba Training Services, a company which evaluates learning packages of all kinds and offers advice to trainers and human resource professionals about the range and quality of training materials available to commercial organizations. There is much in common here with the experiences of setting up such centres in higher educa-tion discussed elsewhere in this book.

As an organization providing advice and information on self-development and training resources, Pba has come in contact with many private and public sector organizations looking for different ways to develop their staff. Over the last two years, the ways of developing staff have changed significantly, from the traditional method of sending people on training courses towards providing them with the learning tools they need to develop themselves. Many organiza-tions feel that there is a dramatic need for a move away from a spoon-feeding approach to that of the ultimate aim of becoming a learning organization, which allows the individual to take full responsibility for themselves and for their own learning. They may also consider such an approach important if they are hoping to move towards achieving the Investors In People award.

CHANGING THE CULTURE

Some sceptics have suggested that this move away from the traditional develop-ment route is purely a cost-cutting exercise. After all, if individuals do become completely responsible for their development, there may seem to be no need for a training department. The more optimistic observer of this shift would see this as a positive step in the whole empowerment process. If individuals are able to take full responsibility for their development, they will take ownership not only for their roles but for their career paths too.

Once an organization has decided to commit itself to such a route, the key is then to provide the means for the individuals to enable them to take control of their development. One such method is by setting up a learning resource centre which can then be accessed by all employees. However, self-development is not a natural process for most of us; after all, we have been accustomed to attending formalized lessons or lectures from an early age, where the environment has been controlled by the teacher and we are conditioned not to necessarily have a desire to learn but to absorb and be reactive rather than proactive. As this process usually continues into our working lives, the paradigm is very difficult to shift.

There is undoubtedly fear and apprehension when any form of change occurs, so when a change in culture around personal and professional development arises, we need to make sure that support and guidance are in place. After all, replacing training with self-development in a resource centre is rather like taking away the feeding mechanism from a child and leaving it to feed itself. The parent does this over a gradual period, but always remains within reach in case the child needs guidance. The same is true of self-development: it is foolish to expect that after many years of learning in a traditional way, people will suddenly have the desire and motivation to develop themselves. So not only do you need to provide support for a self-study mode of learning, but you also need to be able to dispel any fears that individuals may have about the whole process.

ESTABLISHING A CENTRE

Once this movement towards resource-based learning has been initiated for whatever reason, the learning resource centre needs to be established. Unfortunately, many organizations do not put the time or effort required into such a project to make it a successful and, above all, an effective one. This may be for many reasons: lack of commitment from senior management or lack of finance, for example, but in our experience, it usually occurs due to lack of thorough awareness of the entire process. Within this chapter, I would like to set out some of the key issues and provide guidelines for anyone wishing to take this route.

There are many names for open learning centres: they can be known as resource libraries, self-help or development centres. All these terms have the same fundamental meaning: a place where individuals can go to develop themselves and learn. This may be a simplistic description, but when setting up a centre, it is very easy to get lost in the jungle of complex ideologies and jargon. This is why it is so vital to keep this rudimentary objective in mind.

I would like to use the analogy of the launch of a new product to the establishment of an open learning centre. Before any new product is launched, it is imperative that the new idea should be given support from the top. If the support is not there from the beginning, the project can do nothing but fail. It is also necessary to know that sufficient finance is available to back it up; the budget for the centre needs to clearly defined, not only for the initial set-up costs but for ongoing use, staffing, resourcing and updating.

Learning centres do not necessarily have to be a costly affairs; many are set up and run on relatively small budgets. In our experience, a learning centre can vary from a small room packed with resources to a complete floor of a building. Remind yourself that people's development is not worth skimping on and, with a little time and effort, a moderate budget can go a long way, so long as compromises are not made. You do not have to buy expensive videos or invest in all the latest technology, we suggest. Look at what will be most effective for those using the centre and think of their needs; after all, they are going to be your customers. The size of the centre is therefore irrelevant; the most important factor should be how often it is used and whether it is being used effectively. You need to ask yourself, 'Are people we are aiming at benefiting from its existence?'

Once the centre has been set up, how can we get people to come in through the door in the first place, especially as we are aware that it may not be a natural thing for people to want to do? Perhaps even more importantly, how do we satisfy their needs while they are there and keep them coming back?

THE LAUNCH OF THE CENTRE

Awareness of the facility is imperative. The learning centre is there for the benefit of the users and their input should be included from start to finish. After all, the success of the centre will ultimately depend on its usage. The materials contained within it should address the needs highlighted by those using it, as well as addressing the mission of the organization. The launch of the centre should then be geared to the interests of its employees. Many organizations have spent huge amounts of money hiring famous names to attend in an almost party-like atmosphere to unveil their centre, in an attempt to show that their investment in staff exists from the start. It may have little or nothing to do with its potential users.

If these organizations are professing to be investing in their employees, then they should not appear to be short-changing them from the outset by spending on superficial matters rather than on the training itself. Interest has to be gained from the start and fears need to be allayed. The introduction of a learning centre needs to be seen as a positive development and not simply portrayed as a budget cut. The launch provides a crucial opportunity to generate awareness about the centre and raise employees' consciousness about its purposes and facilities. If you can get people interested from the beginning, you are well on the way. It only remains to sustain that interest; in our experience, this is the most complex and demanding part of the process.

ESTABLISHING THE CENTRE'S CREDIBILITY

As we are all aware, the initial euphoria surrounding a new development is soon over and a new and exciting challenge can very quickly turn into a mundane chore. It is similar to the feeling we experience when we go on holiday; for the first two days we explore, we enthuse about the weather and can't understand how we could ever live in England; in the second week the heat becomes a hindrance, the locals may appear rude and incomprehensible, and the food, well, it's just not the same is it? How to sustain interest in the centre is perhaps the most important issue to consider when setting it up. Activities to retain interest can range from monthly newsletters and competitions to physically wheeling a trolley loaded with the latest resources around the various departments, the moral perhaps being if they won't come to you, you must go to them!

Another way of getting staff in to use the centre is by holding events or seminars there. You could invite guest speakers along to talk about a current issue, set up specialist displays, introduce new equipment or programmes or use it for meetings or team talks. This gives people the opportunity to become familiar with the resources and the learning environment.

Most organizations have a marketing department which continually searches for ways of identifying new customers as well as retaining the existing ones. If an organization invests in this process to improve figures on balance sheets, then I propose that the same approach be taken for our internal customers who use the resource centre. People are what make an organization successful, so the investment in them should be of paramount importance.

As many organizations have come to appreciate, simply marketing the centre is just not enough. After all, no matter how much we spend on advertising and mailings, if the product that we are selling is of poor quality and has no value in the market place, we are wasting our time and money. So, before the product is marketed, we need to do our research. It must be established that people want what you are offering, and this leads me to talk about the resources: a centre is only as good as the resources that are contained within it. The difficulty for many organizations has been how to decide what to include, with so many self-study and open learning packages available. Where does one start?

RESOURCING THE CENTRE

The end-user must be kept in mind throughout the entire process. Many organizations have produced in-depth questionnaires to assess everything from individual learning styles to preferences in study media. These self-evaluations are then mailed out and the returns analysed to determine exactly what the employees want, what they need and the range of media that should be on offer. It is important to appreciate that you can not fully address everyone's individual needs and it would be unrealistic to assume that you can. Many organizations consider primarily core subjects or ones which link to their own internally identified required competences. Above all, before you go and buy the resources, we suggest that they be fully evaluated and assessed. No one wants to be responsible for wiping the layers of dust from a product that sounded so good in the promotional literature but was never used.

Technology-based resources

When assessing the resources for the centre, it is vitally important to consider the type of media needed. With a surge in the latest developments as far as media are concerned, particularly in the home market, many of us are accustomed to using a PC or CD-ROM, but how will you know if investing in this medium will be a cost-effective solution to your staff's development needs? This is where the self-evaluation tool or questionnaire will come into play. By looking at individual preferred learning styles, you will be able buy in or create materials to meet the needs of the users. Research has shown that some prefer to learn through going straight into an activity, while others gain more through light reading and familiarizing themselves with the theory, before tackling a particular practical task. We therefore need to provide resources and media which will stimulate and enhance these different learning styles.

If an individual learns more through actively doing (see Phil Race's discussion in Chapter 3) then perhaps an interactive-type medium should be considered, like CD-ROM or CD-I (Compact Disk interactive). From our experience, it would appear that there is a dramatic increase in the interest in these products for self-development and in standard training courses. More and more organizations are setting up 'mini-lab' operations which contain one or more multimedia stations; employees are then encouraged to use the resources on site rather than attending courses. The advantage of this is that individuals can learn at their own pace in a non-threatening environment. If they have not understood something the first time around, there is always the opportunity for them to go back. They can return as often as they like to refresh their knowledge and can pop in for regular updating as new materials come on stream.

The use of videos, we believe, still has an important place in training, as do books and workbooks, yet multimedia seems to becoming more and more used, being so flexible and tailored to self-development situations that it is rapidly becoming a must in any learning centre.

Non-vocational learning resources

Many organizations strongly believe in the value of including non-vocational materials in resource centres, predominantly to aid the whole selling and acceptance process of the centre. Language products may have no direct link with the aims and objectives of the organization, but they are often of great interest to individuals and may entice them in to the centre, where they can then be tempted by other resources available. Making space for materials in the resource centre which are not directly relating to organizational training needs can be a worthwhile investment.

Gauging the usage and value of materials

There may be some areas of development in which you have created a great deal of interest among users. If this is the case, then we strongly recommend that you make sure you have enough resources to cover requirements. This may mean that multiple copies of packages need to be purchased. It is vital that supply meets demand, otherwise the credibility that you have spent so long trying to build with staff will be destroyed in seconds. This is why it is vital that areas of common interest are monitored. Some organizations have adopted or produced complex systems specifically designed to measure usage of certain products in order to eliminate this very problem. Such instruments should make it possible for you to monitor who is using what, so that popular materials can be made fully available to all who want them.

Going back to the product marketing scenario, you should be clear about the characteristics of your target audience, as these are also going to have an effect on the products you hold. Some organizations we have worked with have made the resource centre available for managers only, which obviously limits the viability of such an expensive resource. Inevitably, the user profile will also be a factor in your purchasing decisions.

COMPETENCY OR NVQ MATCHING

Once the users have been identified, their needs analysed and learning styles assessed, the next phase is to determine whether the products are to be linked to NVQs or competences. Many organizations are moving towards competence-based development, looking at behavioural development based on ability rather than pure knowledge, that is, what you can do and how to help you do it better. If the organization does want to relate the materials to competences, the need to evaluate materials becomes even more important. Many resource centre managers do not have either the time or the ability to match available resources to the competences the organization wishes its employees to be able to demonstrate, and compromises are made. This is where seeking a professional adviser who is able to do this for you can be a much more appealing and cost-effective solution.

PROMOTING USE OF THE RESOURCE CENTRE

Once the products have been identified, there is a need to ensure that everyone is aware of their existence, knows what the centre contains and how it works. A list of resources is helpful and highly informative, but does it really guide and support the user? Titles can be misleading. For example, what would you gain from knowing that materials entitled 'The Empty Raincoat' were available to you, if you knew nothing of its content or indeed of its key learning points? (It is in fact about absentee employees who hang a coat in the office so that others think they are there.) This is why many organizations have approached compa-nies like ours to produce a resource manual, on disc or on paper, with in-depth synopses and descriptions of materials to guide the user, making the process of self-development a little easier and ultimately a great deal more effective.

Once the resources have been identified, the environment of the learning centre should be considered. As in training, we are all aware of the pitfalls of uncomfortable chairs, poor lighting, temperamental equipment and so on. If you are serious about the centre and about effective self-development, you must consider the comfort of the users. It has been proved many times that learning is enhanced through the environment and our experience suggests that this is one area that is often overlooked with dramatic consequences. A comfortable, warm environment is highly conducive to the learning process. It usually costs a little more but it is definitely worth the investment.

Maintaining the impetus

The resource guide is one way of promoting the centre and its contents; however, there are many more ways in which a centre can be marketed. Materials can be promoted on a regular basis, theme days can take place to raise interest in a particular subject or issue. Users can be rewarded for their visits by giving them Air Miles or vouchers of some kind, where the organization can support this. Everyone should know where the centre is and how it can be used. All too often, organizations assume that word-of-mouth is a good enough publicity policy to adopt, and all too often their centres remain under-used. You should promote the centre continually, perhaps by using posters and advertisements to get people enthusiastic about the concept.

Once the centre is in existence and the products installed, you should consider merchandising. What you are in effect selling is self-development and the tools by which staff can do this. Resources set out in an attractive and logical way are far more likely to be utilized.

ADMINISTRATION

Having set up and promoted the centre, it needs administering. This area is often overlooked, and the person looking after the centre is also responsible for a million other things. The most effective centres have a full-time dedicated administrator or manager. Many of the most successful open learning centres in industry are operated as a business, with someone responsible for selling the initiative, marketing it and supporting those using it. Most importantly, the person you choose to run it needs to be familiar with the concept of open learning and must be fully able to utilize the media contained within it. With advances in technology, people may be unfamiliar with working with CD-ROM or CD-I and will require advice on its operation. If there is no one on hand in the centre to help them, users will get discouraged and will not come back.

Support and advice from a qualified and experienced resource centre administrator is imperative to the success of a learning centre.

You also need to ensure that the materials in the centre are kept in good condition and are updated on a regular maintenance and renewal cycle. The person you employ to run the centre will need to keep in touch with what is coming on to the market, so they can buy in new materials and replace those that become damaged or dated.

CONCLUSIONS

Setting up and running an open learning centre involves a considerable amount of effort, but the rewards are extremely high. If the process is managed with the end-user always in mind, it can be a very valuable asset to the organization and the individual. The results and benefits will be seen by an increase in motivation and even sometimes a reduction in absenteeism levels.

Unfortunately, mistakes are made, often very costly ones, in terms of cash and credibility. There are many more failures than success stories, in fact. We know of organizations where the usage factor is as high as 60 per cent of the employee base, but the norm is more likely to be a mere 10 per cent or perhaps 20 per cent. Changing a culture of learning attitudes is not an easy one and you will probably encounter a lot of resistance; in our experience, this often comes from those responsible for developing others as well as those using such centres. Sometimes people are frightened of losing their area of specialism, feeling that they have been replaced by technology. In our minds, this is never the case; their roles may change, they may become more coaches and enablers rather than trainers, but the need for their ability is equally as great as that for the right technology. It cannot be emphasized too much that support and guidance are vital and if you have this from the start, the centre cannot fail to succeed.

At Pba, we believe resource centres are here to stay, as a really significant part of the way in which employers can support their staff and help them to continue to be lifelong learners. With a lot of careful planning, sufficient financing, genuine commitment, sensitive market research and perhaps a little expert advice, they can play a key role in every organization's staff and professional development programmes.

Chapter 9

Resourced-based Learning in an International Context

Nick Slope

INTRODUCTION

The subject of resource-based learning at an international level is a vast one. To cover every possibility in such a fast moving field of educational development would not be possible in the single chapter of a book. Therefore, the approach taken here has been to look at principles of involvement and to try and give the reader some practical advice on how to approach international resource-based learning initiatives and how to avoid some of the many pitfalls that await the unwary. The advice given is based on many years' practical experience in dealing with such initiatives that have resulted in many successful, and some unsuccessful, ventures into international resource-based learning.

Within the context of this chapter, the term 'Resource-based Learning' is used to cover a wide interpretation of learning, based on a variety of resources: human, information, and support materials. This broad definition also includes distance, open and flexible learning. Such a wide definition may offend the purist but it allows us to concentrate on the issues surrounding international partnerships, rather than getting hung up on definitions. So whether you intend developing or procuring learning materials for use in your educational establishment, telematically linking with an overseas study centre or setting up an open learning programme abroad, there should be something here for you.

BENEFITS

Many of the pitfalls that can cause international resource-based learning initiatives to falter or fail are discussed below. Indeed the path to success in this area is not easy; if it was everybody would be successful at it. Therefore in order to put success in this area into perspective, listed below are some of the possible benefits of international resource-based learning initiatives.

For *students*, access to:

- overseas students;
- overseas qualifications;
- overseas databases, information, etc;
- cultural diversity;
- international learning materials.

For *staff*:

- professional development;
- access to overseas staff;
- access to cultural diversity;
- research possibilities;
- international dimensions to resource-based learning;
- international dimensions to quality standards;
- access to international learning materials.

For the *institution*:

- internationalization of programmes;
- transnational programme delivery;
- marketing of programmes internationally;
- access to EU funding;
- collaboration in programme design and delivery;
- international certification;
- collaboration in learning material development;
- access to international learning resources;
- added value to existing programmes;
- opportunity to increase income generation.

GLOBAL CONVERGENCE AND RESOURCE-BASED LEARNING

The concept of a global village is becoming a reality. An increasing number of factors, moving at a breathtaking pace, are pressurizing and beginning to mould further and higher education. Commerce and industry have led this global convergence from the first medieval international merchant banks through to today's huge multinational enterprises (MNEs). The move towards global convergence has been transformed from a trend, pioneered by MNEs, to an explosion of international knowledge, information and communication by the rapid and largely unrestricted (and some would say unrestrictable) development of IT. The full impact of the IT knowledge and communication explosion is still largely unknown, but the only real certainties are that the effects will be massive and in many ways unpredictable. Therefore it is essential that those of us in teaching and learning are not left behind but that we recognize and utilize the tools and trends of global convergence and internationalization in pursuit of our primary goal: education and training.

Listed below are some of the primary world-wide trends that are driving education and training towards global convergence:

- MNE expectations of 'international employees';
- acceptance of the concept of lifelong learning on an international basis;
- international growth and acceptance of distance education;
- greater numbers of learners;
- less resource allocated per learner;
- greater diversity of learner profile: age, background, entry characteristics;
- large-scale investment in IT and telematics;
- educational methodological developments in IT and telematics;
- development of learner entry skills in IT and telematics;
- growing acceptance of multimedia and multimedium techniques in education and training.

These international trends, when coupled with the UK educational and training sector's own pressures that largely centre on resource issues set against increased student participation rates, force us to concentrate on the following issues:

- increased numbers of learners;
- flexibility of provision to meet learner needs;
- increased income generation;
- dwindling level of resource per student.

How then do we use global convergence and internationalization to address these issues? In the UK we have two major advantages that make the use of global convergence and internationalism in education and training practicable. First, the international language of the world is English. Second, the UK educational sector has an internationally perceived 'high quality' factor. To this can be added our position in the European network, the innovatory development work in IT and telematics in education and training that has occurred at many UK educational establishments, and the international reputation that we have for distance education. Therefore we can be seen to be in a strong position to use global convergence and internationalization to our and our learners' advantage and to address the issues raised above.

By adopting an internationalist approach we will be able to access and utilize some or all of the following features:

- learner support materials
- learner delivery mechanisms;
- increased student numbers;
- external funding;
- external income;
- international networks.

Given the above perceived advantages of internationalization, why are many educational establishments not pushing harder to develop a wider international resource-based learning strategy for teaching and learning? In my experience, the main reason why internationalization is not used as a major policy tool within many educational establishments in the UK is internal, organizational dynamics.

The difficulties of adopting resource-based learning strategies in an educational establishment, let alone internationalizing that process, are considerable. In most campus-based educational establishments the internal organizational dynamics are set around traditional teaching and learning methods. Assessment, administration, libraries, management, resourcing, staffing, learner support, quality control: all of these fields are usually developed to support a lecture/seminar teaching and learning strategy. To change these systems to support a different, mixed economy of teaching and learning is normally too radical an approach to be contemplated by senior management. Therefore, internal organizational structures remain and new approaches to teaching and learning are grafted onto them. As an example, current staff workloads at most educational institutions are based on contact hours. As a consequence, resource-based learning developments tend to be converted to a 'contact hour' currency that may or may not be applicable to the tasks in hand, rather than a structure developed for staff involvement in resource-based learning activities.

When resource-based learning initiatives are introduced, they tend to put great strain on support systems and are often viewed as 'disruptive' or a 'failure' as a result: they are seen as a threat to existing systems and are judged by system criteria rather than their educational value. Add to these existing difficulties an international dimension that produces its own strains on organizational systems and it is not surprising that international resource-based learning activities are limited to a few educational establishments. There is also a tendency for any activity that includes an international dimension to be viewed as a 'cash cow', with a resultant short-term approach to such activities.

If, however, an educational institution can overcome these particular difficulties and it can be seen that there is a political will at the top of the organization that supports an international approach to resource-based learning, then the rewards are potentially considerable.

FIRST PRINCIPLES

If the decision to proceed in the field of international resource-based learning has been taken, the first question that must be asked is: why? There could be any number of reasons. However, the most common reasons for embarking on such a development are to:

- internationalize an existing programme (added value);
- increase overseas student numbers by franchising;
- gain access to international funding;
- produce commercial income;
- provide access to learning support materials;
- provide access to international networks;
- open international information gateways;
- because it seemed a good idea at the time!

Whatever the reason(s), it is vital to identify them first in order to develop a project pathway and to be able to evaluate the eventual outcome. From initial identification of reasons, objectives can be set and results measured against them.

Having set aims and objectives, the decision has to be made as to what the core of the development is to be. This could range from the acquisition of learning support materials or the establishment of a telematic support network to the setting up of a full open learning programme overseas. This decision will largely dictate where the development is to take place: at home, overseas or conceivably both. Do you intend to be an importer of other organizations' materials, networks, programmes, etc, or do you intend to export your own? This brings us to the question of partnerships: who are you going to work with? It may be that this has already been decided, if for instance there is only one provider of a particular set of learning materials that are being sought. It may also be the case that you already have existing international partners that you could work with.

The next question to be answered is: when are the objectives of the development to be met and/or the development to be operational?

Having established the why, what, where, when and with who, how are you going to achieve your objectives?

PROJECT DEVELOPMENT

Any undertaking that involves the complexities and likely difficulties of an international resource-based learning project requires a project team. It is recommended that there should be an overall project manager, academic representation, technical representation and administrative representation. Depending on the nature and size of the project you may require partner organization representation and external cooptees from such areas as professional bodies and/or from the business or public service communities.

The project team should then draw up a project plan that is owned by the group and accepted by management and academic staff. There should then be regular team meetings with interim feedback on progress.

The overriding question that will have emerged is, how is all this going to be paid for?

FUNDING

There are a number of possible funding routes. The first could be internal funding. Many institutions have curriculum development funds available and some even have commercial development funds. This would probably require some form of internal bidding process. The main problem with an internal route is that sums available are usually quite small and until you have developed a successful track record in development, educational organizations in the public sector are extremely reluctant to provide large sums of cash.

Assuming that you have to take an external route for development funding, there are several sources available. The UK government and some of its agencies will support teaching and learning initiatives that have an international base. The UK KNOW-HOW fund, for example currently supports projects in some of the former Eastern Bloc countries. The British Council and the Overseas Development Agency are also possible contacts. A project that involves industry and/or commerce may well attract funding or other resources such as equipment or staff time from relevant companies.

The next possible funding route is the European Union. This is a particularly rich vein to tap if you are looking at resource-based learning initiatives in Europe. There are several funding programmes for education and training and the EU tends to be very supportive of distance education initiatives. At the time of writing, for Western Europe the SOCRATES and LEONARDO programmes are available for bidding against and the TEMPUS/TACIS and PHARE programmes for Central and Eastern Europe. However there are a number of difficulties associated with these funding agencies, the major one being that they tend to be heavily oversubscribed. The criteria for bidding against tend to be very tight, as do deadlines, and they can be written in a 'Eurospeak' that defies translation.

One way to enhance the bidding process is to be part of a 'club' such as the Open Learning Foundation that has contacts, information and influence, or to form informal alliances with other educational establishments. It is also a good idea to set up your partnerships early to help meet tight deadlines. It is also important that funding bids are put into a strategic, organizational context. As an example, the EU is now moving to ask potential bidders to include their organization's European policy in any bid.

Whatever funding route you decide on, it is crucial to be clear on what you want the money for and what you will do with it if you get it. Many projects that have successfully attracted funding have not reached full potential because, once an organization received the money, they did not have the ability to carry out the project successfully. As an example, many EU bids require that the bidder provides 'matched funding' on a 50/50 basis; if you attract such funding, you must be certain that you can meet such criteria. The advice is:

- be clear on what you want from any funding;
- ensure that it is set in a strategic context;
- make certain that you can match any funding requirements;
- do some footwork on what is available;
- set up partnerships early;
- get to know the 'wrinkles'.

Another resourcing issue is the maintenance of any project. Some educational establishments have accounting systems that may not effectively match income against expenditure. As an example, you could be generating income with a healthy surplus but find that your establishment's budgetary controls do not allow you to spend money in, say, upgrading out-of-date materials. It is vital, if a project is to carry on post-external funding, that any maintenance and support costs are budgeted and allowed for. A proper business plan should cover this area.

So you are now clear on what you want out of your project, how you are to go about it and how it is to be funded. What issues are you likely to encounter during the project development that make an international resource-based learning venture different from others?

CULTURE AND COMMUNICATIONS

Much ink has been spilt in attempting to define exactly what culture is. Hupchick (1994) defines it as:

> the way a particular group of human beings (a society) adapts to its physical and human environment.... Culture provides groups of humans with their collective self-identity, thus shaping their every activity and institution.

The essence of culture as it applies to this topic is that people in different societies can have different perspectives, values and expectations. This means that for international resource-based learning initiatives to succeed there must be a fundamental understanding, on both sides, that cultural differences exist. Indeed, there would be little point in developing such initiatives if this were not the case.

One of the first things to accept when dealing with other cultures is that teaching and learning is a cultural activity. Therefore, it is dangerous to make assumptions about what is transferable from one culture to another. As an example, tutoring is a very culturally based activity and different cultures approach supporting learning materials very differently. Assessment strategies can also be very different from culture to culture so it is important to consider the teaching and learning processes that partner-staff and students are part of.

In most cases, the first cultural obstacle to be encountered is language. Language difficulties can occur at all stages of a project, but can be most damaging if they occur at the initial stage, particularly in the understanding and interpretation of what both sides expect to gain from such a project and how this is to be achieved. Therefore, it is essential that all parties are quite clear on what expectations and development mechanisms others have at the outset of any initiative. If the initial perceptions of what is to be achieved and how it is to be done are different at the start of any development, then stormy waters lie ahead. It is highly recommended that contracts and/or written agreements are drawn up and agreed by all parties, clearly defining roles, responsibilities, development and delivery mechanisms, outcomes, financial conditions and any other requirements deemed necessary for the success of the undertaking, prior to any project commencement.

The development of any resource-based learning material that contains text should be considered carefully. An example of what can go wrong in this area was encountered by me when project managing the development of an open learning workbook, in English, for use in South East Asia. One of the workbook authors, in a laudable attempt to try and 'contextualize' the material, used oriental names in case examples. Unfortunately the names were taken from a newspaper that was reporting the trial of some oriental gangsters. The result was a series of villainous Chinese nicknames punctuating the case examples that caused quite a stir when they were revealed. Fortunately, the quality control mechanisms that had been put in place picked up the offending names and they were changed. The lesson is that, even if you are writing in English, you should make certain that quality control mechanisms are in place that will scrutinize the cultural elements of language, as well as any direct translation that may take place. We are most of us aware that the word 'rubber' has a different meaning in the UK than it has in the USA, for example!

It is even more important that language and cultural issues are considered in the development of assessments where a student misinterpretation of an exam question, for instance, could have serious implications.

In an age where English is the prime medium of communication at an international level, it is easy to assume, as a native English speaker, that because someone talks and listens to you in English that they understand you and that you understand them. As Archie Bunker, in the American TV series, said to his wife: 'Ethel, either you're talking in English and I'm listening in dingbat or you're talking in dingbat and I'm listening in English!'

We are all products of our environment and possess preconceptions and stereotypes of other cultures. It is easy for us to assume, for instance, that South East Asian cultures are very similar to each other. It is equally easy for someone in South East Asia to assume that all Europeans are very similar. However, cultural differences can be very strong in areas of geographically close proximity: take the former Yugoslavia as a good example. Therefore it is dangerous to assume that because something works well in one area that the same will apply elsewhere. International resource-based learning initiatives should treat each new venture with the care that you would the first. Even if culturally a new partner may be similar to a previous one, their academic processes may not be. Try putting yourself in your partners' shoes and seeing how you may look to them.

Provided you have ensured that all parties are clear on outcomes and processes, most of the problems that occur at a cultural level will be unforeseen ones. A military maxim states that 'no plan survives contact with the enemy' and while in no way should partners be seen as 'enemies', the maxim holds true. Problems will occur in the best laid plans and you should be prepared to deal with them. As an example, during the setting up of a text-based open learning programme in a former Soviet country we discovered to our dismay, having set up a desk-top publishing facility to produce master copies of translated workbooks, that there was no paper available to print the workbooks on. In order to deal with this type of situation, there needs to be a flexibility of approach, an acceptance that things will go wrong and that there will be a steep learning curve, on all sides, before such initiatives bed down and run smoothly.

One certain method of destroying goodwill between people of different cultures is to offend them. Insensitivity, flippancy, assumptions of superiority and arrogance lie at the heart of many failed international initiatives. Often people are not actually being insensitive, superior or arrogant: they just appear to be so. Sensitivity to others and how they may perceive your attitude to them is a vital component of successful international developments. It is essential to make certain that staff involved in such developments are careful not to offend. Making religious or political jokes may be an obvious thing not to do, but it is surprising how often this can happen in an unguarded moment.

Cultural differences can cause difficulties at the most unexpected times. Following a three-week training programme for some overseas staff on developing flexible learning, we produced an evaluation sheet for participants to fill in. The result of the evaluation was superb: every category listed was given top marks. While this was very flattering it was clear that the result was a 'thank you' from the participants rather than a true evaluation of the programme. We then handed out new evaluation sheets and explained to the participants that, in order to help the next group of learners it was necessary to have a 'true' evaluation. The participants then dutifully filled out the new sheets and the result was dreadful: every category was given bottom marks. The participants were telling us what they thought we wanted to know; we had not explained clearly to them why they were completing the exercise.

In fact, the above exercise was a failure to communicate rather than a cultural misunderstanding. Much is blamed on cultural misunderstanding that is, in reality, down to poor communications. Setting up effective lines of communication is very important in the development of an international initiative. You will save much heartache by doing so, and by ensuring that partners receive answers to queries quickly. Quick response times can be very difficult to maintain if you are working for a large educational organization. In order to answer a question regarding academic processes, for instance, you may have to go to an academic board or equivalent. This could cause significant delay. Therefore, it is suggested that you contact your partner immediately, explaining the reasons for any delay and giving a date when the query will be answered.

The area of culture and communication is a sensitive one that requires considerable thought and effort to get right, but if you get it wrong it can be the death of any international project. In summary:

- all parties accept that cultural problems will arise;
- all parties understand what they hope to achieve from a collaboration and how they are to achieve it;
- a contract/written agreement is drawn up that defines roles, responsibilities, financial obligations and any other requirements;
- all parties understand their partners' cultural teaching and learning context;
- a quality control mechanism is in place that will check text for cultural problems as well as translation;
- you and the staff involved avoid the assumption that because you speak the same language you understand one another;
- you and the staff involved avoid the assumption that geographical proximity equates to cultural similarities;
- flexibility of approach is developed in order to handle cultural and communication problems;
- you and the staff involved are sensitive to other cultures and are seen to be so;
- effective lines of communication are developed;
- a timed response system to enquiries is set up.

PARTNERS

One of the most crucial aspects of setting up any international resource-based learning initiative is the choice of partners. If you have existing partners that you have worked with before and are happy to work with again, then all well and good. If, however, you are looking for new partners, then take care. The road to hell is littered with failed international projects due to the wrong match of partners. The way not to find partners is to jump on a plane and set up agreements with the first people you meet. This may seem too obvious a point to labour but it does happen.

If you are looking for partners in Europe, it is useful to be part of a network such as the European Association of Distance Teaching Universities (EADTU) and/or European Distance Education Network (EDEN). For instance, at the time of writing, EADTU has established a considerable number of Euro Study Centres (ESCs), both campus-based and distance/open universities, across Europe that are telematically linked using the First Class Desk Top Conferencing facility. This facility allows ESCs direct contact with one another, enabling partnerships for resource-based learning initiatives to be established quickly and to be focused on mutual capabilities and needs. If you are looking for partners in Central and Eastern Europe, then the PHARE network mentioned earlier is setting up central contact points in these countries.

If you are looking further afield then it might be useful to contact agents that have established partners already operating in the country you are interested in. Organizations such as the Association of Commonwealth Universities may be able to assist in finding suitable partners in specific areas. Local contacts such as the British Council may also be able to assist you. It is also worth getting in touch with embassies and consulates for contacts.

However you locate your potential partner(s), you will probably need to check them out. In the first instance this is best done informally, to see whether it is worth proceeding to a more formal stage. If your informal check is positive then the next stage is to draw up a draft agreement and business plan, from which you should be able to establish exactly what each of the potential partners is looking for out of a relationship. Assuming agreement by all parties, a formal agreement should then be drawn up. If you are looking to franchise programmes or courseware, any agreement should be followed by some type of formal validation.

In summary:

- devote much time and effort to securing the right partner;

- use existing networks, agents and organizations to help focus your search;

- check out potential partners informally if you are at all uncertain about them;

- ensure that all partners are clear on what they hope to get out of any partnership;

- arrange for a formal validation if franchising programmes;

- draw up formal agreements.

QUALITY ISSUES

As stated above, I believe the single most difficult problem that faces an educational institution seeking to develop and initiate new teaching and learning strategies as well as international partnerships, is the organizational structures and dynamics that are already in place. These structures have normally been set up to service full- and part-time students based on a lecture/seminar teaching and learning strategy. This can be particularly true of quality mechanisms. As an example, the academic calendar of an international partner organization may be different to your own. You therefore need to ask yourself whether you can organize an exam board to suit their students if this falls in August, for instance, when most academic staff are not available. Below, there is a discussion of some of the quality issues that, in my experience, it is wise to take into account. Clearly the level of approach and consideration will differ according to the scale of the international resource-based learning initiative concerned.

One of the most important and difficult areas of quality concerns assessment. An early question to ask yourself concerning an international resource-based learning initiative is: is there a requirement for an assessment strategy to be put into place, either for your home-based students or for the overseas students? A number of factors are indicated below. This is offered as a guide to the sort of questions that you may have to ask yourself when trying to develop, service and maintain an international resource-based learning assessment strategy.

Strategy

Is assessment to be by:

- examination
- coursework
- project
- portfolio?

Will it be:

- continuous
- computer-based
- formative or summative?

Timing

- The academic calendar
- academic staff availability
- administrative staff availability
- external examiner availability
- the arrival/dispatch of scripts
- exam boards
- notification of results
- appeals?

Administration

- How much will it cost?
- How will assessment be logged?
- How can security be ensured?
- What will be the procedures?

Assignment setting

- Who will set the assignment?
- What will the quality control procedure be?
- How will cultural and linguistic checking be ensured?
- What will be the nature of partner involvement?
- How much will it cost?

Sitting assessments

- What will the language of assessment be?
- Will the students be working in English as a second language?
- What will the timetable be?
- What will the environment of sitting be?
- How will security be ensured?
- How will extenuating circumstances be dealt with?

Marking

- Who will do it?
- Will it involve double marking?
- Will there be partner involvement?
- How will marking be undertaken securely?
- How will feedback be given?
- What will be the mechanism for external checking?

Exam boards

- What will the composition be?
- What will the constitution be?
- Who will be the externals?
- Where will it be held?
- How will extenuating circumstances be dealt with?
- How will the results be published?
- How will student progression be monitored?

Awards

- How, when and where will certificates be printed?
- What arrangements will be made for awards ceremonies?

The above list is in no way to be taken as comprehensive but as a starting point. Many difficulties can arise over relatively minor issues. For instance, the name that goes onto a certificate: should it be in Latin or Cyrillic script? Should it contain a patronymic? Which is the family name and which is the given? All of these questions may have to be addressed.

Validation

Another quality issue is the validation, if required, of any resource-based learning material and/or programme. How does a particular initiative fit into the validation structure of an educational establishment? Validating panels need guidance on what is good practice and what is not, or else you are likely to run into difficulties during the validation process. There are a number of publications available that can assist in this area; for instance, the Higher Education Quality Council has recently published a guide to collaborative provision that can be obtained direct.

How a particular international resource-based learning initiative is to be supported academically, pedagogically, administratively and how it is to be managed are all important quality issues that must be addressed. A large number of support issues revolve around staff development. This is a crucial quality issue. How you involve and develop both academic and non-academic staff will be crucial to the success and failure of any international resource-based learning initiative. There is also an issue concerning the ability of students to cope with such initiatives. Introducing, for example, a new international desktop conferencing network has implications for student development as well as academic, technical and administrative staff development. If students are not trained in the use of technical equipment or shown how to analyse critically vast amounts of information, then it is likely that such a project would fail.

CONCLUSION

The development of resource-based learning initiatives in educational establishments is normally a difficult enough process in itself without the added complications that an international dimension gives. However, the greater the difficulty, the greater the reward. Successful international resource-based learning initiatives can produce very positive benefits for the staff and students involved, as well as benefiting institutions in such areas as learning material development. But the route can be quite rocky and there are many pitfalls. Some of the major issues, in my experience, that affect the success or otherwise of international resource-based learning initiatives, have been discussed here. These discussions will hopefully provide guidance for those involved, or wishing to become involved, in this area of development. As I have indicated, it is not possible to look in detail at all the various types of international resource-based learning initiatives. The approach adopted here has been to highlight general issues.

So, when considering an international resource-based learning initiative you should:

- make certain that you have set clear objectives and that they are understood by any partners;

- ensure that you are clear what your partners' objectives are;
- take care in the selection of your partners;
- draw up an unambiguous contract/written agreement;
- ensure that any initiative is properly resourced;
- make certain that any conditions of funding can be matched;
- prepare for and expect cultural and linguistic misunderstandings;
- set up clear lines of communication with any partners;
- establish effective quality control systems for the checking of any text-based material;
- ensure that institutional quality control systems can cope with such initiatives;
- make certain that effective support systems are in place;
- ensure that staff and students can cope with such initiatives.

Following the recommendations made in this chapter will not guarantee success, but will assist in the development of rewarding partnerships. There are two key aspects of any collaborative agreement with overseas partners that will greatly promote the development of resource-based learning initiatives. First, all involved should be treated as equals and any collaborative venture should be seen as a partnership of equals. Second, any collaborative venture should be developed with a view to a long-standing relationship between partners that will reward staff and students of all participating organizations.

REFERENCE

Hupchick, D P (1994) *Culture and History in Eastern Europe*, London: Macmillan Press, p.5.

Chapter 10

The Implications of Resource-based Learning for Libraries and Information Services

Charley Hardwick

In 1994 the Oxford Brookes Centre for Staff Development organized a series of seminars and workshops on the subject of resource-based learning (Brown and Gibbs, 1994). Each one examined resource-based learning initiatives in the context of a broad discipline area: different events covered, for instance, art and design, the built environment, the sciences, and so forth.

For the Library and Information Service (LIS) at The Nottingham Trent University, the series seemed to offer a major opportunity for its faculty liaison officers and information specialists to learn about the latest resource-based learning developments. With this in mind, each of the seven or eight events in the series was attended by the appropriate member of LIS staff accompanied by, wherever possible, a member of staff of the corresponding faculty who was active in the resource-based learning sphere.

The seminars and workshops gave an excellent overview of a range of developments across higher education, but it was difficult to detect the way in which the majority of them would make radically new demands on libraries and information services. In many cases, it is true, the curriculum developments called for changes in resourcing and resource management that might require libraries to make operational and strategic changes, but the nature of these was usually such that they could be accomplished within traditional boundaries of staff responsibilities and service practices. The Copernican shift implicit in resource-based learning, which suggests that the resources used will exert a major influence on the way teaching and learning are accomplished, appeared not to have had a revolutionary effect on libraries. Yet at a time when the universe of information sources is expanding so dramatically, and when references to transferable skills and independent learning are commonplace, this seemed strange.

I intend to investigate this emerging universe, and its relationship to resource-based learning, by describing a number of case studies, many of them using examples from work being done at The Nottingham Trent University. They will demonstrate different approaches to resource-based learning but, in two areas in particular, the studies take us away from systems and orientations that perhaps tend to characterize libraries in their more 'traditional' roles, where well-established operations and familiar practices are simply adapted in order to support resource-based learning.

The case studies have been selected with a view to focusing attention on what seem, to me, to be three highly significant resource-related issues: first, what are the resources students will be expected to use; second, where will they use them; and third, how will the resources be used? The identification of resources, the 'what' question, is illustrated by describing library input to an initiative that forms the basis for a chapter elsewhere in this book. An examination of the 'where' issue takes us out of the library to look at student use of networked information services across the campus. Finally, we shall focus on a first-year module that is designed to teach students 'how' to use information sources effectively and efficiently. Needless to say, the three studies are not mutually exclusive.

CASE STUDY 1: WHAT RESOURCES?

Andrew Charlett's contribution to this book (Chapter 7) describes how resource-based learning is used to support learning on a part-time BSc (Hons) Building course which has minimal attendance requirements. This section will look in detail at the contribution made by the LIS to this initiative. We shall see that an extremely successful venture, which involved teaching staff in writing a series of units to support a flexible system of independent learning, made extensive (but not new or innovative) demands on LIS and its staff.

The chief involvement of the LIS Information Specialist for Building has consisted of working closely with the course team in order to confirm the current availability of 'required', 'recommended' and 'referred' texts, and to check that these have been accurately cited in the units. Where it is felt inappropriate for the students to rely on commercial suppliers for access to particular texts, LIS has advised on other strategies for making them available. These have called for, among other things, reviews of library loan procedures, careful exploitation of such reciprocal access arrangements as still operate between libraries in the higher education sector, and offering advice on copyright procedures.

The last of these areas, copyright, takes us beyond the experiences of any one university, and opens up a debate on an issue of national importance to an educational system that sees resource-based learning as one strategy for coping with larger numbers of learners. Copyright considerations present us with a complex legislative framework that controls access in both print and electronic formats. The legislation frequently works against our ability to make multiple copies of texts available in ways that will not only be financially attractive to hard-pressed budget holders, but also relevant to the pedagogical aims of course teams.

When responding to these pressures in the context of printed sources, librarians have been inventive in adapting and developing conventional materials and services. The most frequently used strategy involves the establishment of short loan collections, either as physical entities or through changing the loan categories of materials in the main collections. In either case, texts can be moved in and out of short loan or reference-only sections to meet the needs of particular courses at particular times. It goes without saying, however, that any new stock management approaches must succeed educationally as well as economically, and the chances of achieving the former will be greatly increased if librarians and lecturers work closely together.

While cooperation was a key factor in prepackaging the distance learning version of the part-time Building degree at Nottingham Trent, the particular approach adopted by the course inevitably places limits on the extent of the day-to-day contributions made by the LIS. While LIS responded positively to requests that identified texts should be made available for the students during their occasional periods of attendance at the university, ranging from once every two weeks to once in four, other possibilities which would shift the debate about LIS support firmly into the areas of where and how resources are used, were thought less relevant to the needs of this particular course.

However, in the case of the 'how' issue, the information specialist does provide both induction and, for final year students preparing their dissertations, information skills sessions. Even so, the content and timing of the latter are strongly influenced by the 'what' approach to learning resources. This means that while the skills session aims to give a full understanding of how, for instance, a CD-ROM database is used, the approach is more mechanistic than would be appropriate in a course where the nature of the project work requires students to develop their abilities as independent information-gatherers at an early stage. In such contexts the aim is truly to develop transferable skills that will benefit the student not only throughout the course, but also in later life; and a strong case can therefore be made for encouraging critical and evaluative orientations to research tools as learning resources. As we have seen, these were significant but not major considerations with regard to the distance-learning degree in Building. The issue is, therefore, developed later in this chapter in connection with another course at Nottingham Trent.

The next section deals with the 'where' issues implicit in resource-based learning.

CASE STUDY 2: WHERE TO ACCESS RESOURCES

In 1995 LIS collaborated with the university's Computing Services staff in establishing pilot 'learning rooms' in two different faculties. Among other facilities, the rooms would provide IT workstations giving access to LIS services, available over the network, including CD-ROM databases and networked access to JANET and the Internet. This development is intended to support three objectives (Lines and Griffiths, 1994):

- To extend the range of facilities available to support student learning.

- To encourage and facilitate innovative approaches to structuring the learning experience outside the classroom.

- To pilot possible arrangements for (future) learning facilities.

Although it is conceivable that the last of these objectives could influence future developments of the university's library infrastructure, the rooms are clearly seen as providing opportunities for collaborative, resource-based study in distributed learning spaces, where it may not be feasible for library and computing staff to offer other than a very occasional presence. Along with their teaching colleagues, however, such staff are being encouraged to investigate and initiate innovative uses of the facilities offered. This has resulted in at least one joint venture between library and teaching staff, in which the Information Specialist (David Fisher) and the Course Lecturer (Sue Hallam) have taken the lead in an exercise with Health Studies students that involves the creation, use and evaluation of Web home pages (Fisher and Hallam, 1996).

The emergence of the Health Studies project, and many of a similar nature in other universities, raises the question of the degree to which our existing university libraries provide either suitable or appropriate 'learning space' for a diverse range of resource-based activities. Certainly there is nothing intrinsic in the use of the Internet as an information source which suggests there is a need for it to be consulted in a library. Link this factor with others – growing pressure on study space; catering for both silent and conversational learning activities; providing adequate facilities for training students in resource-based learning-related study skills; accommodating IT-based study – and the case is strong either for distributing learning spaces around the campuses, or for replacing many of our libraries with new buildings that can cope with the emerging demands of resource-based learning.

Debates about the degree to which library services should be centralized or distributed (or the merits of physical compared with virtual provision) were a thread running through the recommendations of the Follett report (Follett, 1993). In the section on information technology, references to old libraries being 'given over to parking' and to 'access not holdings' provide somewhat dramatic underpinning to the decision to make funding available, through the Joint Information Systems Committee (JISC), for a range of projects under the 'electronic libraries programme'. These cover seven key areas, many of which are of direct relevance to the interlinking issues of what resources are available and where they are best accessed. The area covering access to networked resources, for instance, includes projects that, on a much larger scale, mirror the work of Fisher and Hallam at Nottingham Trent: examples include the University of Bristol's work on the Social Science Information Gateway (SOSIG), and the EEVL project (the Edinburgh Engineering Virtual Library).

Despite the fact that there are approximately 40 electronic libraries projects currently supported by JISC funding, new library buildings are being planned that, for the foreseeable future, will have to accommodate physical as well as electronic resources. This suggests that planners need to be aware of some of the issues raised earlier, and that they should consider providing facilities that reflect ongoing developments: project rooms for group access to resources in a range of formats; enquiries areas capable of handling in-depth queries involving a technical/bibliographical intermixture; and purpose-built training accommodation for information skills tuition.

In many cases the planners will be helped by information emerging from the JISC projects, three of which relate to the issue of how students will use resources. These are NetLinks, based at the Department of Information Studies at the University of Sheffield; NetSkillS, a project based at the University of Newcastle upon Tyne, which provides a training programme aimed at shifting the culture in higher education towards effective use of networked information resources; and EduLib, which plans to provide a nationally recognized network of library and support workers who will possess both the network information skills and the teaching skills required to make the use of electronic libraries an everyday part of teaching, learning and research.

CASE STUDY 3: HOW TO USE RESOURCES

Within The Nottingham Trent University's Department of Building and Environmental Health, the honours degree in Environmental Health includes two modules that adopt mechanisms for developing professional skills and encouraging reflective practices, that are process-based and problem-centred. They are run in the second and third semesters under the generic title 'Trent Health Department' (THD), which has as its central aim the development of 'professional skills though all years of the course'. Both THD modules have the added function of integrating and interrelating the core subject knowledge taught in other modules on the course. In the interest of brevity I shall refer to them here as THD/1 and THD/2. It is THD/1 that will be of main interest, since the skills with which it is chiefly concerned are those associated with the efficient and effective use of information sources.

In the second semester of the first year (THD/1) this is largely achieved by having students undertake a project exercise that places a strong emphasis on developing their confidence and independence as users of a wide range of information-gathering and research tools. (A detailed account of this approach appears in Hardwick and Hooper, 1996.) In the context of this chapter we shall focus specifically on the nature of the involvement of the LIS through the contribution made to THD/1 by its Environmental Health information specialist.

The information specialist is particularly involved at two crucial stages in the life of the project, and variously at times during the ten or so weeks in which the students are undertaking their research. The two crucial stages are, first, presenting the aims of the project exercise to the students and, second, assessing the process elements of the project work. In between, as will be seen, the information specialist takes on a tutoring function at seminar group sessions which are built in to the THD/1 timetable. I shall begin by looking at the assessment arrangements.

If a central objective of a resource-based learning approach is that students should acquire transferable skills in the areas of resource use and exploitation, then it would seem appropriate overtly to assess the acquisition of those skills in some way. This view is shared by the Environmental Health course team, and has resulted in 40 per cent of the THD/1 marks being allocated to the processes of topic selection (20 per cent), bibliography compilation (5 per cent) and the submission of a detailed research report (15 per cent); with the remaining 60 per cent being awarded for the substantive subject content of the finished project. This means that while the information specialist is present at the topic selection seminars, in order to steer students towards choosing research areas that are well resourced, his main assessment activity involves marking the final research reports.

These reports are submitted on specially designed pro formas. A questionnaire approach is adopted to elicit reflective and critical responses from students regarding the sources they have used (CD-ROMs, current awareness services, directories), and their approaches to the research process in general. Since the initial project presentation session will have included advice and guidance on maintaining a research record (for which a separate set of pro formas is supplied), the completion of the report will draw on the thoughts and observations students have noted down throughout the project exercise. The reports will, therefore, allow the information specialist to monitor and evaluate the nature and level of the learning that has taken place, and to give feedback to the students at the final seminar group debriefings.

I will turn now to the project presentation stage and the tutoring activities of the information specialist. The vital element here is cooperation, as it is throughout THD/1. All sessions that relate in any way to the process/product interrelationship are jointly presented by the course lecturer(s) and the information specialist. It is particularly important to adopt this approach at the initial project-setting sessions, since the students do need reassuring that an account of a research exercise that carefully reflects on problems is, at this stage in their course, probably more valuable than one that records straightforward solutions. This fact is further reinforced at the jointly run, non-obligatory, drop-in 'clinics' that are offered to seminar groups at two stages in the project schedule. At these events, students are encouraged to air their thoughts and concerns about any aspect of the project exercise.

Since 1996, the tutoring possibilities have been extended by offering access to a specially established e-mail discussion group. This provides an open forum for, specifically, the THD/1 group of students, their course lecturers, their information specialist and a member of the university's Teaching and Learning Enhancement Centre. At this stage the aims of the e-mail link are more modest than the extensive use of 'networked learner support' envisaged by the JISC-supported NetLinks initiative. Fowell and Levy (1995) refer both to networked delivery of information skills training, and to '"just-in-time" guidance to learners as they carry out their project... work'. For now, however, the THD/1 discussion group will basically facilitate timely comment and intervention by lecturers, fellow students and the information specialist and, before it takes on the wider training role, it may be used in its present form in connection with work at THD/2 level.

In the second year, students will be required to undertake an in-depth critique of a selected source. At present, it is accepted that this will probably be a non-electronic text, but it is recognized that an opportunity opens up here for students to use databases, available via both BIDS and the Internet, to contextualize their chosen source in terms of others related to it. This is a good example of the interplay between, on the one hand, resources and learning, and on the other, between lecturers and librarians.

AFTERTHOUGHTS

Any case studies approach has its strengths and its weaknesses: it allows an observer to lay a pattern over a range of activities where there is, as yet, no apparent structure; but it also imposes rigidities and artificial boundaries at the most inconvenient times. In the case of libraries and resource-based learning, the 'what', 'where' and 'how' issues cannot be divorced from one another, but allowing them to mix produces a complex cocktail of issues. For example, the relationship between commercial information providers and a higher education sector needing to manage resources for growing numbers of learners will affect curriculum design, the planning of library accommodation, and the nature of the skills the learners will need.

This complexity, while it has stimulated so many initiatives, also indicates that, for librarians at least, we are at a pre-paradigm stage. Where Follett (1993) suggests that we should 'go with the flow, and paddle like mad', the actualities are that the current is sweeping librarians into areas where many of us feel stimulated and challenged but, at the same time, wary and ill-prepared. Getting to grips with rapid and complex changes in the availability of information sources is fine, and advising on how these can best be accessed presents new challenges, but, as we rise to these challenges, experiments with resource-based learning draw us into debates that impact on course planning, computer network management and skills for learning.

As we hit the white water (but continue to discourse phlegmatically on the fact that we have not been schooled in the pedagogical issues implicit in designing a learning experience that promotes reflective and critical thinking), we notice here a lecturing colleague and there a computing services specialist, bobbing along beside us. And we realize, as we hope other colleagues do, that no one group or agency has the wherewithal to ensure that resource-based learning will be effective. So while we pray that all colleagues will reach calmer water, we wonder if by then any of us will be wearing the same life-jackets or sitting in the same boats.

ACKNOWLEDGEMENTS

My grateful thanks to Andrew Charlett, Ann McCarthy and Liz Lines for their various contributions to this chapter.

REFERENCES

Brown, S and Gibbs, G (1994) *Course Design for Resource-based Learning: Built environment*, Oxford Brookes Centre for Staff Development.

Fisher, D and Hallam, S (1996) Unpublished material in reference to their work with BSc (Hons) Health Studies students at The Nottingham Trent University.

Follett, Sir Brian. Joint Funding Councils' Libraries Review Group (1993) *Report [for the] Higher Education Funding Council*, London: Higher Education Funding Council for England.

Fowell, S and Levy, P (1995) 'Developing a new professional practice: a model for networked learner support in higher education', *Journal of Documentation*, 51, 3, 271–80.

Hardwick, C W and Hooper, J (1996) 'Watching the detectives: developing students' analytical and evaluative research skills', *Improving Student Learning*, Proceedings of the Oxford Brookes 3rd International Symposium. Oxford Brookes Centre for Staff Development.

Lines, E and Griffiths, I (1994) Quoted with permission from an internal memorandum written by Liz Lines, Head of LIS, and Ian Griffiths, Head of Computing Services, both at The Nottingham Trent University.

Chapter 11

Integrating Multimedia Resource-based Learning into the Curriculum

Bernard Lisewski and Chris Settle

INTRODUCTION

Resource-based learning is underlain by the philosophical assumption that allowing the learner to achieve learning outcomes in a more flexible and independent manner is inherently better than the traditional learning method-ology, epitomized by the 'banking' concept of education criticized by Friere (1972). The debate on the empowerment of the learner is a difficult one to resolve. The main difficulty is that, initially, learners may not be in a position to decide whether or not empowerment, in its various degrees and manifestations, will equip them for a given learning task.

Learner empowerment must involve a more equal relationship between the teacher and student, with an acknowledgement that the teacher is not the sole provider of subject knowledge. Facilitating rather than dictating the learning process, there is also a requirement on the teacher to provide an enabling structure within which learners, especially those new to subject domains, are able to develop learning independence.

In higher education recently, part of this enabling structure has been the formulation of learning outcomes which attempts to highlight the learning to be achieved. The great danger of this is academic prescription, balanced against the need to provide a learning pathway for students. Just as important is the requirement for assessment practices which both match desired learning out-comes and provide students with the opportunity to demonstrate that they have achieved such outcomes.

The application of resource-based learning within a learning outcomes sce-nario raises certain questions. First, what type, availability and mix of resources will best allow the learner to achieve the specified learning outcomes? Second, how should the learner use the resources in order to achieve the desired learning outcomes efficiently? Third, how do we know how the learner is using the resources to achieve the learning outcomes?

These questions will be answered differently depending on both the content and the context of the learning. For example, resource availability (favourable student/computer workstation ratios) and operational logistics (access times to learning resource centres) are, in our experience, just as likely to determine the success of resource-based learning initiatives as educational design.

The teacher and the learner must feel at ease with the resource-based learning initiative, particularly when using the new technologies. This 'comfort factor' requires appropriate staff development structures for teachers and induction to resource-based learning on behalf of learners. With regard to the use of multimedia, teachers and learners still vary from being 'hardened cybersurfers' to 'technophobic neurotics'. The latter innocents have even been known to use the 'mouse' as both a 'remote control' unit and a 'foot pedal'.

DESIGNING APPROPRIATE LEARNING ENVIRONMENTS

The effective integration of learning technology into the curriculum depends more on the need to design appropriate learning environments for students than on producing a delivery medium *per se*. Harrison (1994, p.30) has argued that:

> Learning technology is not chiefly concerned with using computers, video recorders, audio tapes or any other form of technology. Rather, it is concerned with a systematic approach to the planning and delivery of the educational experience. In other words, it should be more concerned with the design of the whole learning experience than with any particular delivery medium. From good design, it should become clear how best to deliver a quality learning experience.

Similarly, Laurillard (1993, p.220) has highlighted the importance of context of delivery when integrating different media formats into the curriculum:

> The development of media-based materials is important, but delivery is paramount. The most stunning educational materials ever developed will fail to teach if the context of delivery fails. Conversely, good delivery can retrieve poor materials. The 'context of delivery' means more than a delivery system, such as lectures, mail or broadcasting. It refers to the provision of whatever support it takes to enable students to achieve the maximum benefit from their study.

IMPLEMENTATION ISSUES

Our discussion on the integration of resource-based learning into the curriculum draws heavily on students' experiences of using multimedia learning materials, as the major form of course delivery on a year-two 'Weed biology and control' module within the school of biological and earth sciences at Liverpool John Moores University (Lisewski and Settle, 1995a). The rationale for the innovation was a desire to offer students greater access to the subject content, increased flexibility in their times and pace of study, and the opportunity to develop more autonomous methods of learning, while at the same time providing them with a reasonably structured learning experience. Laurillard (1987, p.50) has emphasized that: 'computer based training be pedagogically appropriate for its intended use'.

The learning technology adopted, a multimedia CD-ROM format, provided a linearly structured body of information alongside stated learning outcomes. The learning materials replaced a series of 20 one-hour lectures. Students had access to a dedicated suite of 12 free-standing Macintosh Centris 650 machines (with attachable CD-ROM drives) from 9am to 5pm, Monday to Friday within a 13-week semester. The module began with an induction meeting where students were introduced to the learning package. Interspersed within the module were four one-hour time management seminars at which students could raise concerns with regard to their use and understanding of the materials. Use of the learning materials was tracked electronically, thereby allowing the two tutors to monitor student study times and patterns.

EVALUATION STRATEGY

Resource-based learning innovations should undergo critical evaluation. The authors believe that the more traditional educational delivery methods, such as the lecture, should also be subject to equivalent critical gaze. In observing the performance of learning technology, Draper *et al.* (1994) state that:

> what must be studied is whatever has significant effects on learning; this is not just the technology or the medium, but the educational intervention as a whole.

Evaluation is not a straightforward activity and there is not one best method of undertaking it. An action research perspective in the form of an illuminative evaluation, as espoused by Parlett and Hamilton (1977), is recommended as the best strategy. The primary aims should be to describe and interpret what happens within the social-psychological and material environment in which students and teachers work together rather than trying to objectively measure and predict the learning outcomes.

We have demonstrated elsewhere (Lisewski and Settle, 1995b) the importance to the evaluator of:

- developing good working relationships with the academic/technical staff and students;

- negotiating confidentiality agreements and data reporting procedures with participants;

- planning evaluation schedules.

Evaluation should be a collaborative exercise which is undertaken in the interests of all those engaged in the teaching and learning process. For example, teachers should be involved in the evaluation exercise and as such be made to feel that they have sufficient ownership of it. Evaluation should improve the learning package, and its associated learning environment, on the basis of student feedback. The evaluation tools can take the form of:

- questionnaires;
- continuous student diaries;
- semi-structured interviews;
- an electronic tracking system.

In designing and using these instruments in the evaluation of learning materials, it is important to bear in mind Reeves' (1992) maxims that:

- it is difficult and probably futile to evaluate outside the context of use;

- individual differences among users with regard to previous experience, expectations of learning and motivation etc must be accounted for in any evaluation;

- interactions among these individual differences and aspects of the user interface should be a major focus for an evaluation.

Underpinning any evaluation strategy should be the perspective that many factors affect the outcomes of learning, not least the assessment methods employed within any teaching and learning context.

BALANCING STRUCTURE AND EMPOWERMENT

Resource-based learning which replaces a sequence of lectures presents students with the difficulties of motivating themselves and organizing their time. Two students' comments illustrate the problem of managing their time within a less formally structured learning environment:

> When there are deadlines to be met every other day, it's all too easy to leave this until all else is done. I know this is a disciplinary problem on my part but my lecture attendance is usually good. If there are lectures, I do make time for them as I hate getting behind in a subject.

> Took notes, finally finished. Got it all out of the way, before the work piles up after Easter. Good idea to have it on the CD-ROM, you can do it in your own time. But you have to make yourself do a bit each week, otherwise I can imagine you have a lot to do at the end of the term when you've got all your other work, so you have to be disciplined.

Achieving the correct balance between a structured approach to learning and personal empowerment is a difficult one for students to gauge. Mere availability of resources for learning does not guarantee that learning will take place. As well as learning to manage their time, students need specific guidance on how to use learning technologies efficiently and effectively. Rowntree (1992, p.100) argues that:

> Even with the most everyday media (let alone with high-tech approaches) you need to teach your learners how to learn from the medium before you can teach them anything else with it.

Similarly, Jacobs (1993, p.2) has stated that any learning technology must exhibit the important quality of transparency:

> Above all... good practice assumes that users of learning technology are able to concentrate on learning without (necessarily) thinking about the technology, since if the technology cannot be made to work transparently, actual practice will at best lag behind ideal practice, and at worst be abandoned altogether. Impatience is a barrier to learning, and particularly if it is the result of struggling with the learning tools themselves. If the teacher or learner is constantly having to tweak the technology, or ending up with a half-baked implementation because the setting-up process has proven too difficult, the learning tool may well be left to gather dust.

With these thoughts in mind, it is important that students are inducted into the proper use of any given learning technology along with guidance as to how to manage their time. You should devote as much attention to how learning materials are used as to how they are presented to students. Peer-group support mechanisms should also be encouraged where difficulties in the subject matter can be addressed.

JUSTIFICATION FOR THE USE OF THE TECHNOLOGY

Teachers need to be very 'up front' with students as to why a particular technology is being adopted within the curriculum. If lectures are being replaced by a multimedia package, then the benefits of this should be spelled out to the students. One may wish to emphasize, for example, the flexibility of use of a multimedia package in that students should be able to work in their own time and at their own pace. Below are some student comments on how they used our learning package:

> The student can take as much or as little time to learn one particular part of the course. Therefore he/she can spend more time on the subject matter which he/she is not so familiar with.

You are able to use the package when you want. You are also able to proceed at your own pace, and re-cap things you've not understood. Can be used during gaps in lectures.

You fit your sessions into your college timetable so that you don't have to come in especially to do the module.

Can work at own pace if disciplined enough or if had experience of using it in the first year which would be an advantage. Information is always there, lectures can miss a lot.

THE ROLE OF THE LECTURER IN THE LEARNING ENVIRONMENT AND INTERACTION

Within any resource-based learning initiative, students need to be clear as to what the role of the lecturer is and what forms of learner support are available to them. Students place great faith in lecturer availability, need to put a face to a name and want to have the opportunity to question their tutors. Whether or not, for example, a piece of software is effective may depend as much on the nature of the human support as it does on the technology.

Students are well aware of the problems of not participating in the traditional face-to-face lecture situation. For example, they miss the verbal and visual cues of the lecturer. The following students' comments are indicative of this:

It has been suggested that an advantage of this type of course is that if you do not understand a concept you can go back and examine it again. However, since the computer cannot re-word the concept the probability is that you will not understand it any more the second time. When a lecturer is explaining a concept that the students find difficult, he/she will usually pick up on the blank faces and present the concept in a different way.

In some cases, no matter how many times you read something it still makes no sense. In a lecture situation if something is not understood, a lecturer will re-word what they are trying to get across. This is not the case when studying from the computer. No real problem has yet really occurred that hasn't been sorted out with fellow students but it could.

MONITORING PATTERNS OF STUDENT USAGE

It is important to monitor patterns of student usage of learning packages. Ideally, this should be done via an electronic tracking system. An example of the type of information which can be obtained is illustrated in Figure 11.1. This data allows teachers to:

- monitor student progress through the learning package;
- examine student study strategies;
- provide study guidance to future students;
- plan future computer requirements on the basis of capacity usage.

Student Reference: 93032137
Date: Monday, April 3, 1995
Session Commenced at 1:24:31 pm
Section opened: Module 3 Section 3
Time: 1:24:38 pm
Section opened: Module 3 Section 4
Time: 2:53:14 pm
Section opened: Module 3 Section 5
Time: 3:24:44 pm
Session ended: 3:25:42 pm

Figure 11.1 *Electronic tracking data*

SOME POTENTIAL PITFALLS

Hawthorne effects

In assessing the 'success' of multimedia learning packages, Kulik and Kulik (1991, p.88) state that one has to take into consideration what they call the treatment effect of computer-based instruction (CBI). This they argue is related to length of treatment:

> CBI was especially effective when the duration of treatment was limited to four weeks or less.... It is unclear, however, why effects are significantly smaller in long studies. A novelty effect, or Hawthorne effect, could certainly explain the finding. A novelty effect occurs when learners are stimulated to greater efforts simply because of the novelty of treatment. As the treatment grows familiar, it loses its potency.

Widespread use of multimedia formats may increasingly test students' comfort zone of acceptability. The important staging-post will be how to integrate computer-based delivery across the curriculum, while at the same time, maintaining the students' engagement and interest. One could realistically argue that this is equally the case with traditional lecture-based delivery methods, charismatic lecturers with a dramatic sense of theatre being the exception rather than the rule!

Dangers of prescription

In any resource-based learning initiative, there is always a danger that students may perceive the learning package as being the only prescribed dose to be taken for the successful completion of the course. One student's comment is indicative of this:

> Usually you have to go chasing after books – but this was formatted for you, lots of structure for you, everything provided for you. You still have to apply yourself and organize your time but you are not library book-chasing all the time.

Clearly there are trade-offs for the student: the dangers of a self-contained learning experience may be offset by the time saved by not having to pursue subject matter sources from a variety of other reference points. There are two competing forces at work here: on the one hand, there is the potential danger of prescription in that students regard any multimedia learning package as all there is to know about subject x, while on the other hand, the courseware may act as a traction facility to pull the students through the subject content.

Another issue is whether the idea of multimedia courseware is in fact an impractical oxymoron of little relevance to higher education provision. For example, Fowler (1995) argues against what he calls the 'courseware culture club', emphasizing that multimedia should be used principally as a visual medium to aid conceptual understanding in difficult areas and not as a straight replacement for the lecture or the book. This argument, however, does not get us round the problem of how to deliver quality mass higher education in an age of a falling unit of resource, something which the Teaching and Learning Technology Project (TLTP) has vainly sought to address.

ASSESSMENT AND FEEDBACK

Periodically, students require signals and reassurance that they are on the right track. This potential anxiety raises many issues, paramount amongst them being the importance of assessment and feedback in determining how and what students learn. This highlights the need to:

● provide formative feedback to students, as to their progress through learning packages;

● redesign the assessment methodology in line with new approaches to teaching and learning.

As Laurillard (1993, p.218) states:

To ensure materials are properly embedded into a course, re-think the assessment in the light of new types of learning inculcated by new teaching materials and methods.

Senior management support

The continued support of senior management is essential if any innovation is to be resourced effectively and its momentum maintained. Clearly, the greater the degree of support that an innovation can gain, and the wider its institutional influence, the better will be its prospects for success and development. Castleford (1995, p.xi) has placed particular emphasis on the need for this:

Successfully implementing computer-assisted learning materials into the curriculum requires nothing less than a change in the teaching culture. If IT is to play an effective role within higher education all the members of that community need time not only to reflect on which applications are both feasible and desirable, but also to devise and implement effective, integrated and appropriate strategies. This demands, at least, the active participation and co-operation of lecturers, heads of departments, deans, Pro-Vice Chancellors, and Vice Chancellors.

World Wide Web (WWW) platform

Whalley (1995, p.25) has recently emphasized the limitations in the use of CD-ROMs:

No expense or difficulties in running them (especially networked) but, by their nature, they are inflexible even if they do provide hypertext linkages. They also suffer from the same pedagogic disadvantages as books, they are expensive and cannot be updated readily. I believe that they are best left as storage media for data, records or as dictionaries, encyclopaedias etc. They have a place but it is restrictive and will probably remain so for many teaching purposes, despite advances which will soon provide 2–3Gb, rewritable CD-ROMs.

Unsurprisingly, Whalley continues by advocating the use of the more easily publishable, updateable and networkable WWW as a flexible local and distance-oriented teaching and learning tool. Student expectations are mainly that it is the teacher who will be able to guide learners through the huge amounts of information that are currently available from various media sources. This is particularly pertinent to the technology of the lecture, where the learners are increasingly the masses. The romantic vision of students browsing through fields of knowledge, gathering an education as they go, does not sit easily within the need to provide students with an enabling system of learning. For example, claims that 'Teaching on the Internet is learning' (Pickering, 1995) need to be treated with some caution. On-line publishing media such as the WWW may offer more and more information but the danger is that they may provide less and less meaning. The problem, of course, is that while all this 'educational cybersurfing' might provide an electronic playground for learners, students and teachers alike, we might equally be in danger of 'amusing ourselves to death' (Postman, 1986). At this stage, we just wish to 'flag' a cautionary note about this, nothing more. At a minimum, we have to equip students with the ability to separate the important from the trivial.

The use of on-line learning materials within the curriculum also places a great onus on an institution's ability to guarantee student access to these resources. One student comment neatly underlines this problem but alternative delivery platforms such as the WWW are likely to set the agenda in the future:

> It was not computers as I usually see it. With networked computing, etc there are always 110 things going wrong. The CD-ROM format was very user-friendly which is a contrast to the network.

CONCLUSION

For multimedia resource-based learning innovators, the basic questions remain: what is the appropriate use of the medium and what type of learning is being fostered by its use? These are course design issues concerned with the integration of learning technology into the curriculum, the matching of learning outcomes to relevant learning opportunities and assessment methodologies, and the role of the tutor, other than information-provider, within technology-based learning environments.

As a general observation, resource-based learning innovators need to ask the question, what learning resources are we creating for the envisaged learning environment within which we wish our students to study? It is not just the production and design of the materials *per se* which is important but the design of appropriate learning environments.

ACKNOWLEDGEMENTS

We would like to thank the students for their honest and constructive feedback. Our thanks also go to Andy Young, Roy Stringer, Peter Kelly, Peter Fowler and Professor Peter Wheeler. The Esmee Fairburn Charitable Trust granted financial support for our project and Holt Studios International provided the still photographs for inclusion in the learning package.

REFERENCES

Castleford, J (1995) 'Drowning in marking and time for a sea change', *THES* Multimedia Features, June 9.

Draper, S W, Brown, M I, Edgerton, E, Henderson, F P, McAteer, E, Smith, E D and Watt, H D (1994) *Observing and Measuring the Performance of Educational Technology*, University of Glasgow TILT Project Report.

Fowler, P (1995) 'Challenge to the courseware culture club', *THES* Multimedia Features, March 10.

Friere, P (1972) *Pedagogy of the Oppressed*, London: Penguin Books.

Harrison, C (1994) 'The role of learning technology in planning change in curriculum delivery and design', *ALT Journal*, 2, 1.

Jacobs, G (1993) 'Standards', *ALT Journal*, 1,1.

Kulik, C L C and Kulik, J A (1991) 'Effectiveness of computer based instruction: an updated analysis', *Computers in Human Behaviour*, 7.

Laurillard, D (1987) 'Introducing computer based learning', in Thorpe, M and Grugeon, D (eds) *Open Learning for Adults*, London: Longman.

Laurillard, D (1993) *Re-thinking University Teaching: A framework for the effective use of educational technology*, London: Routledge.

Lisewski, B and Settle, C (1995a) 'Teaching with multimedia: a case study in weed biology' *Active Learning*, 3, December, 28–35.

Lisewski, B and Settle, C (1995b) *IT in Teaching and Learning: A staff development pack*, TLTP project video: Developing an Evaluation Study, Durham University *et al.*

Parlett, M and Hamilton, D (1977) 'Evaluation as illumination: a new approach to the study of innovatory programmes', in *Beyond the Numbers Game*, Basingstoke: Macmillan.

Pickering, J(1995) 'Teaching on the Internet is learning', *Active Learning*, 2, July, 9–12.

Postman, N (1986) *Amusing Ourselves to Death: Public discourse in the age of showbusiness*, New York: Viking Penguin.

Reeves, T C (1992) 'Evaluating interactive multi-media', *Educational Technology*, May, 47–52.

Rowntree, D (1992) *Exploring Open and Distance Learning* (1st edn), London: Kogan Page.

Whalley, W B (1995) 'Teaching and learning on the Internet', *Active Learning*, 2, July.

Chapter 12

Setting up a Resource-based Learning Centre for Staff to Provide Guidance and Support on Teaching and Learning Issues: A Case Study

Sally Brown, Tina Carr and Dorothy Bell

INTRODUCTION

Many institutions of higher education in the UK and elsewhere are reviewing the means of provision of support for their staff, particularly as we are striving to demonstrate that we take issues of teaching and learning seriously within our quality assurance mechanisms. Many staff and educational developers are discovering that it is increasingly difficult to encourage attendance at courses and events when there is more and more pressure on staff in difficult times.

Resource-based learning for staff can be cost-effective and very successful when it provides ways for staff to access materials and resources at their own convenience. This chapter explains how a dedicated resource centre which is appropriately stocked, equipped and staffed can be invaluable for those who wish to keep themselves abreast of current developments in teaching and learning. Here we describe how this has been achieved at the University of Northumbria at Newcastle (UNN) and we offer some advice for those who might wish to provide something similar in their own institution.

What is MARCET?

The Materials and Resources Centre for Education and Technology (MARCET) at UNN is a learning resources centre which supports the university's academic staff with resources and services to help them to develop innovative teaching, learning and assessment practices. It also makes available to administrative and technical staff a range of resources to enable them to support academic staff and promote enriched student experiences as well as to develop their own professional expertise.

MARCET is part of the university's educational development service (EDS) and is located within the service in a central position in the university's city centre campus. It comprises a large room containing books, magazines, journals, videos, resource packs and other materials. We have a range of equipment in MARCET for use by MARCET staff and clients. This includes Apple Mac and PC computers, video playback facilities, laminator and binder. Staff are encouraged to use our facilities to produce their own high quality teaching and learning materials and MARCET and other EDS staff can provide advice and training in the use of this equipment. At the heart of the operation are the staff: information officer Tina Carr, information assistant Dorothy Bell and students on placement, currently Paul Thompson. Line management is the responsibility of Sally Brown, educational development adviser.

Background of MARCET

MARCET was established in 1990 in response to the demand for high quality resource materials stimulated by the Enterprise in Higher Education Programme (EHE) at UNN and the centre was sponsored by EHE, the library and the EDS. MARCET was always based physically close to the EDS and became a permanent part of the department when UNN's EHE contract came to an end in October 1993.

MARCET: a learning resource centre for staff

It was always the intention to establish a learning resource which not only contained books but also provided resources in other formats on teaching, learning and assessment themes. MARCET provides a warm, friendly working base and our clients find it very convenient to be able to consult everything they need in one place. They are able to browse through journals and then access other electronic information sources via the Internet. They have access to the professional experience and expertise of MARCET's staff as well as the team of educational development advisers, and they can discuss their particular needs in a quiet, comfortable environment. They can use the MARCET facilities to produce teaching and learning materials and can refer to other textbooks and open learning packs in the centre for inspiration and ideas.

MARCET finance

The initial funding to set up MARCET came from two primary sources: the EHE initiative and the (then) Polytechnic's Development Fund. Enterprise funding could only be used for staffing and to provide books, journals and subscriptions, while the development fund provided the furniture and computer hardware. In addition, the EDS, which at that time was quite separate from MARCET, provided pump-priming funds for the first bulk order of books to establish the centre.

With the conclusion of enterprise funding at UNN, the cost of running MARCET came within the budget processing system of EDS. EDS is one of the university's central departments, and bids annually for both revenue and capital funding. The estimated expenditure for the running of MARCET is itemized separately within the EDS budget. When the annual budgets are agreed with finance, MARCET is allocated an amount for books, journals, software, educational packages and subscriptions to CD-ROM databases out of the department's allotted revenue budget. The day-to-day running costs of print and reprographics, stationery and hospitality are covered by the general EDS budget.

In order to purchase capital equipment (as opposed to maintenance revenue), we have to review the effectiveness of the equipment we are using at the time and assess our future needs. We aim to provide a rolling programme for maintenance and replacement over a period of years. However, the allocation of capital equipment to MARCET very much depends on the priorities of the EDS as a whole. The new developments to expand MARCET, described later, have been funded centrally, as it is part of the university's mission to provide flexible and effective staff development for all categories of staff.

THE SERVICES MARCET CAN PROVIDE

Advice on information sources

The centre has a range of information sources in different formats including journals and abstracting journals, CD-ROMs such as ERIC and International ERIC and access to electronic information services via the Internet and World Wide Web (WWW). These supplement the collection of books, open learning packs, videos, audio cassettes on teaching, learning and assessment themes and management and self-management topics, most of which can be borrowed by UNN staff.

MARCET staff can carry out literature searches on topics of interest and can advise clients on which material best suits their particular needs. Training for users is provided as needed in the use of information sources, particularly electronic sources so that they can easily find what they want within the centre.

Keeping staff informed through *Education Update*

This newsletter started out as a brief current awareness news sheet, aimed at academic staff and containing references to articles of interest in the educational development literature. Over the years it has evolved and now contains news items about things going on in the EDS, and short abstracts are attached to each journal reference. We are now considering producing *Education Update* in other formats on a more regular basis and are exploring the WWW as a vehicle for dissemination.

Databases

We already have available for staff a number of databases, for example on NVQs, and we are acquiring an increasing number of databases in CD-ROM format. We are also collaborating with colleagues in our central information services department to make best use of networked CD-ROMs. We are able to access many information sources via the Internet and are trying to find ways of bringing to our clients' attention useful areas on the WWW.

Links with academic advisers

A valuable aspect of MARCET's work is that it can link the casual inquirer to the expertise of the team of academic advisers who work in the EDS. This means that if someone comes in looking for material on self- and peer assessment for example, not only would they be directed to the appropriate reference material, but they would also be asked whether they would like to talk to one of the academic advisers who have expertise in this area. This is a two-way process, in that staff consulting the advisers are often brought into MARCET to be given relevant *Red Guides* (our own brief and friendly in-house publications for staff by staff) and shown books, journal articles and other relevant material.

Internet and WWW

MARCET aims to help staff to keep abreast of technological developments in teaching and learning. We currently have available a Power Mac 7100/66 which is connected to the Internet giving us access to all services to JANET and particularly the WWW. As the centre develops, we intend to offer further facilities through which staff can discover how best to use the WWW for teaching, learning and assessment.

We have a home page for EDS which enables WWW users to access details of MARCET and to find out about our publications. This is located at http://www.unn.ac.uk/~edu8/

We find this valuable, because it helps to publicize our services both internally and externally and will provide opportunities for on-line interaction, for example, in relation to conferences mounted by EDS where we plan to have pre- and post-conference discussion groups. University staff who wish to use the Web are also making wide use of the facility in MARCET as they may not have other access to it.

Events

We hold around six MARCET events annually, including seminars and a larger-scale one-day event focusing on, for example, open learning, resource-based learning and using technology in teaching and learning. The seminars are designed to increase awareness of what resources and expertise we have to offer, with a prime purpose to increase the constituency of our institutional users. Our full-day events are usually open to both UNN staff and external visitors, and include speakers, displays, workshops and seminars, with a strong emphasis on opportunities for hands-on experiences of resources and technology.

The UNN has campuses in Newcastle city centre, three miles away at our Coach Lane campus, and a number of hospital sites following our merger with a large local nursing college, as well as at Morpeth in Northumberland and at Carlisle in Cumbria. Recognizing that MARCET is based on only one of the university's sites, we aim to take display material out to the other sites and to organize some of the events on at least the bigger campuses.

Visitors and external users

MARCET has attracted visitors from all around the world who want to see what we have on offer, often with a view to setting up a similar resource centre of their own. It is always worthwhile to welcome visitors, even though it is time-consuming, as we are able to benefit from their external perspectives and expertise. It also provides us with opportunities to attempt to sell them some of our publications.

UNN's library has reciprocal arrangements with other academic institutions such as Newcastle University: staff from other universities are welcome to browse through all our materials, but we cannot offer them all the services that are available to our own staff, for financial reasons.

Similarly, although we permit students, particularly postgraduate students, to use the resource centre in order to view materials, we have to restrict usage, particularly of the computers, to staff.

MARCET AS A PUBLISHING HOUSE

It has always been a key aim that MARCET would be a channel of dissemination of good practice within and beyond the university. From the start, we aimed to act as a small-scale publishing house, initially encouraging our own staff to write about their successful projects that were funded in our institution through EHE. Subsequently, we have encouraged staff to write about aspects of their experiences of teaching, learning and assessment. Our main channels of publication are *Red Guides* and *Castles Guides*. We also offer occasional special publications like our survival guides for students travelling to study in Europe and we act as external sales agents for some other UNN publications, such as study skills materials for arts students.

Red Guides are small, A5, paper-covered publications, usually not more than 2,000 words long, offering practical advice and based on personal experience. We encourage the writers to adopt an accessible, jargon-free style rather than what you would find in a formal refereed journal. Although many of our authors are widely published, we also encourage new lecturers on our Post-Graduate Certificate in University Teaching and Learning to make good use of the research undertaken for their projects through writing a *Red Guide* based upon their findings. *Red Guides* are provided free to all members of staff who want them and are sold externally individually, in themed packages and by site licence. Profits thus generated are ploughed back into the production process.

Castles Guides are A4 in format, of greater length and substance and often comprise edited collections of, for example, papers from our own conferences or outcomes from our activities through which we celebrate alternative approaches to teaching and learning.

Organizing publishing through the publications committee

The MARCET publications group includes MARCET staff and representatives of departments and central services. Meeting approximately six-weekly, we review the progress that has been achieved on the publications on the stocks and consider the new proposals that have been suggested to us, as well as considering what other topics might be suitable for our list and who might write them for us. Once a proposal has been agreed, it gets listed on our grid and assigned an agent. It is the job of the agent to check and report on progress, to give first-line editorial advice and ensure that the completed work is of a sufficiently high quality. The text is then transferred to the MARCET information assistant for desk-top publishing. We cannot pay our authors, but provide them with five free copies (and a master copy, if required).

All our publications carry ISBNs (International Standard Book Numbers) which is one of the means by which we encourage our staff to write for us. Particularly for inexperienced staff, *Red Guides* often offer a first route for external publication. As a publisher, MARCET can allocate ISBNs to its own publications. When an ISBN is issued to a book, a book information form must be completed and sent off to Whitakers. Information on the form is distributed to booksellers and librarians all over the world, and eligible book information is supplied to the British Library's Cataloguing in Publication programme. This means that our material is in the public domain and can be found on book lists and a variety of electronic databases, which in turn leads to improved sales.

A copy of each publication is sent as is required to The Legal Deposit Office in The British Library and a further five copies are later requested by the other five legal deposit libraries via the Agent for the Copyright Libraries in London.

We find it a great benefit that we can enable our authors to become more widely known through the accessibility of their publications, and it also helps to generate interest in our publications and MARCET itself.

Distribution and sales

A copy of each *Red Guide* is given to all heads of department within the university, who are encouraged to inform their staff about them. We also list new *Red Guides* in the university's internal newsletter and in our own *Education Update*. In order to generate the funds to be able to supply staff of the university with *Red Guides* free of charge, we sell our publications to other institutions. Details of all our *Red Guides* and *Castle Guides* are listed in a catalogue which is produced twice a year. Each new catalogue and order form is sent to educational and staff development centres throughout the British Isles. Recently we have included information about the guides on the MARCET Home Page on the Internet and trust that this will lead to further enquiries.

The distribution and sale of guides is administered entirely within MARCET. This came about because it was proving too costly for the university's finance department to raise invoices for low amounts (currently £1.50 per copy). We ask for prepayment, ie cheques with order form, and can supply pro forma invoices if requested. Sales of publications are held in a publications account which operates independently of the MARCET revenue account.

ORGANIZATIONAL STRUCTURES

In order to ensure that we provide the right kind of service for the staff of the university, MARCET is guided by a steering group that comprises representatives of the faculties and central services. The group meets three times a year and has advisory and supportive functions. We also make considerable use of our contacts in the departments, formally and informally, to find out what people need from us.

As well as depending upon the established team, MARCET makes use of students on placement and work experience to undertake appropriate duties. This has been a particularly fruitful and cost-effective source of staffing: students from diverse backgrounds such as business studies and computing have worked with us for periods up to a year giving us specialist help with marketing, Internet literacy and the organization of events.

Assuring quality: monitoring usage and service

We are able to monitor how our centre is being used in a number of different ways, both quantitatively and qualitatively. A daily record is kept of who visits the centre, why they have made the visit and for how long. A similar procedure is followed for telephone requests for information. We try and gain user feedback in order to measure the effectiveness of our services and facilities, via question-naires, feedback sheets, observation, and informal discussion. We are also aware of the population of non-users in the university and are actively pursuing ways of reaching this group in order to find out what the barriers are that prevent them from using our services. Our quality assurance mechanisms lead us to believe that those who do use us find MARCET particularly valuable not only for the facilities we can provide but also for the services we offer.

THE FUTURE: A VIRTUAL MARCET?

At the time of going to press, we are currently doubling the size of MARCET and enlarging its user constituency to include much more support for allied staff at the university, as well as academic staff. We are using the occasion to relaunch MARCET as a centre much more focused on technology for teaching and learning, since this is an area of rapid development, as resources shrink and tutors are increasingly looking for new methods of course delivery. Many staff and educational developers believe that an important element of such developments will be the increasing use of technologically supported learning. The new MARCET will provide facilities to come in to try out a wide range of packages from all kinds of sources and to develop confidence and expertise in their use.

The way in which the centre is used is changing also with a greater emphasis on independent study, with all categories of staff able to use teaching packages and resource-based learning materials on site. This will make our services more cost-effective and will satisfy the need to be flexible in our provision. Alongside the much-larger MARCET will be a second room flood-wired so that we can move portable computers through and connect them to the university's network for small-group training. For the rest of the time, they will be available in MARCET for individual use.

Our university has also expanded in recent years from two to eleven sites, and we recognize that a service based on the city centre campus cannot hope to serve our campuses at Coach Lane, Carlisle, Morpeth and a number of hospital sites around the city. We are therefore investigating ways in which users on all our campuses can utilize our services on-line in the most effective manner. We anticipate wider use of e-mail, the WWW and teleconferencing.

LEARNING FROM EXPERIENCE: KEY ISSUES

In this section we aim to review what we have learned in the setting up and running of MARCET in the hope that our experiences will be of benefit to others planning to do the same. The advice we offer is based on what has worked for us, as well as on some of the less positive experiences we have had, when things have not gone as well as we had hoped.

Staffing

We have learned that a major stumbling block to the successful operation of a resource centre is insufficient staffing. To be of real use to staff, the centre needs to be open and fully functioning not only during the standard working period, but also at unsocial hours (so staff can pop in before and after work and in vacation periods). This has been a significant difficulty which has only been partly ameliorated by strategic use of our part-time staff, involvement of academic advisers and creative use of students on placement. On occasions we have been embarrassed to find that we cannot provide the service we wish, for example, at times of staff illness or holiday. We hope this will be further remediated once the new MARCET becomes fully operational, as then we will gain additional support from information services staff who can offer us additional specialized support, particularly with technology for teaching and learning.

At the moment we are a small, close-knit team, willing to roll up our sleeves and help out in times of crisis. As the centre grows and the range of services offered is extended, it is inevitable that our team will grow and become more diverse, so much of the communication and planning that is currently done informally may need a tighter structure. In particular, an operations manual is being developed to enable all staff working in the centre to provide a first-class service.

Resources

An important learning point for us has been the need to budget not only for the purchase of materials and equipment, but also for maintenance, updating and consumables (toner, paper, etc). It is not wise to purchase IT equipment and then find there is no one available to install, maintain or repair it. The centre has been well endowed in the past: the challenge now remains for us to bid for and receive sufficient funding to allow us to grow and develop.

Technology

MARCET is intended as a showcase for the best materials and equipment available, so that staff can find out about what they can use to support their teaching and learning and can try it out at a convenient central location. However, we are continually coping with the tension between our wish to provide the newest and the best materials and our need to keep within budgetary limits. Others wishing to set up similar resource centres will need to budget accordingly. One way forward is to explore the possibility of loan equipment from suppliers and manufacturers who could be convinced that having their equipment on display in such a centre would contribute to sales.

Keeping up to date

Staff working in a resource centre need to continually update their own expertise, not only through courses and conferences, but also through informal means such as visits, work-shadowing and placements. In MARCET we have gained enormous value from the specialist knowledge of our computing student on work placement who has quietly and sensitively helped us all to climb the difficult IT learning curve!

Security

Any resource centre will be vulnerable to theft, both intentional and unintentional. All our loan material has to be issued through the university on-line library system and we have to be extremely careful about people who want to borrow material for the odd hour and then forget about it. An additional problem is that issues can only be made by the trained staff and not by, for example, the placement students who are often in sole charge. We cope with this through a temporary issue system.

To prevent more criminal disappearances, we have to ensure that the room is secure, alarmed, not available for casual use and never left open unattended. Although this makes us more inflexible in our availability, it ensures that we hold on to our stock. This is important when we have thousands of pounds worth of computers and books on site.

CONCLUSIONS

We are understandably proud of MARCET, feeling it is in the vanguard of development of open access resources for university staff. We have learned a great deal in the process of setting up and developing the centre, and its mission and establishment have changed as the needs identified by staff have changed too. We are interested in exchanging experiences with colleagues in similar resource centres and we welcome visitors by appointment. However, be warned: if you come to see MARCET you may well leave lighter of pocket once we have sold you some of our publications, and heavier of heart from envy at what we have achieved here.

Chapter 13

Evaluation and a Culture of Learning

Mary Thorpe

An edition of the *British Journal of Educational Technology* in 1995 carried a series of articles on the 'new' technology now being introduced across education and training everywhere, including the UK Open University (UKOU), where the context might be described as that of a 'traditional' distance teaching institution. It seemed appropriate to raise the issue of whether we should 'pity the poor student' in this new world of high tech learning and low staff:student ratios (Thorpe, 1995). Although many might see the UKOU as already in the vanguard of technology-led learning, inside the institution there is still a strong ethos of student-centred teaching and learning. It is appropriate therefore to question the new technology just as we have evaluated the effects of the old, and the key question remains the same: are these technologies, as they are applied, in the best interests of students? Do they raise or lower the quality of their experience, not least the quality of their learning?

We shall each discover different answers to these questions in our own institutions, no doubt influenced by the latest impact of government funding and its effects on our own strategic direction. Do these same questions apply to resource-based learning? I believe so: resource-based learning need not be technology-led, but the expectation that learners can study effectively, independently from tutor-led face-to-face teaching, raises essentially the same issues of whose interests are being served and the effects on learning.

However, I would argue that the increasing use of resource-based learning using innovative technologies is having a progressive outcome in one sense. It has generated renewed interest in student learning among teaching staff. Staff are curious about what these technologies are and some at least are eager to learn what they offer teaching in their discipline. There are exceptions to that generalization of course, but I can only speak of the context I know best. At the UKOU, teachers experienced with 'old' technologies of text and audio/video come with a willing suspension of disbelief. They are wisely sceptical but interested and, on occasion, excited by some of the opportunities that multimedia and computer-supported learning may open up for us (Mason, 1994).

None of the technologies of the Internet and the convergence of computing and telematic media were part of the experience of the vast majority of university

130

academics, concentrated as they now are in the age range of late 40s and upwards. Few of us bring intuitive ideas about what it could be like to learn with the new media, derived from our own lived experience as students. And for many of us, some of our most taken-for-granted assumptions are challenged at their roots (Whalley, 1995). We have never had to consider before, for example, that narrative – the development of a story line or chronology – is central to many ways in which we deliver our curriculum in practice. If multimedia resources made available to our students on the Web or via CD-ROM technology require something other than the conventional narrative 'line' (Laurillard, 1995), then what is our alternative and how are we to teach?

This is but one example of the challenge to us as teachers that we now face and I believe the self-questioning is having a positive effect in my own context, if only because it leads so directly into discussions about how students learn – using both 'old' and 'new' technologies. Resource-based learning does not necessarily use new technologies of course, but for those new to it, it surely poses the same questioning about how we are to teach using new methods and what assumptions we are making thereby about how our students will learn.

THE IMPLICATIONS FOR EVALUATION

The need for evaluation in this context is usually readily accepted, if only on the grounds that where there are new methods, the results must be documented and assessed. Furthermore, since students study independently of face-to-face contact, evaluation is required to find out what exactly the 'input' has been. How much of the text or program/CD-ROM has been read? What amounts of study time were required, and what is the range across the course population, in terms of workload, interest level, perceived difficulty, and so on (Chambers, 1995; Rowntree 1994).

In the case of a technology such as computer conferencing, the course interactions can be saved in an archive that represents a documentation of what the course has been for a particular student population, without requiring further data collection. However it still needs analysis to check out different levels of participation across the students, and the extent to which educational goals were being achieved, through content analysis of conferences (Wegerif, 1995).

Is this the only purpose for evaluation? Is resource-based learning a happy opportunity to increase the number of posts for researchers focused on the issue of 'did the course deliver what it set out to do?' I do not wish to challenge the need for such evaluation; on the contrary: any activity which legitimizes outcomes-based course evaluation is welcome in my view, and checking whether students achieved the goals as set is an essential and not an optional role for evaluation. I do want to argue however that a rather more ambitious agenda for evaluation should be taken forward. We should not confine evaluative effort solely to the level of course-by-course quantitative data-gathering.

Distance education, as one version of resource-based learning, has many examples of evaluation used to explore the wider social context of teaching and learning, including in-depth analyses of learner response to materials, at a level of detail which can contribute to research into student learning (Evans, 1994; Morgan, 1993; Thorpe, 1995). I have identified three major focuses across this range of approaches: curriculum and values, the learning environment, and empirical studies of materials in use, and each is discussed in turn.

CURRICULUM AND VALUES

Distance education, as one of the forerunners of resource-based learning, has always been challenged by those who would argue that it risks offering a pre-digested and spoon-fed curriculum. Harris, in one of the earliest such critiques, argued that the wish to create conventional standards and comparability with the rest of UK higher education, competed with the ideology of openness at the UKOU and created a closed rather than an open curriculum for its students (Harris, 1987).

Harris has subsequently argued a modified view, in relation to in-service courses for teachers. As a tutor of Masters courses for serving teachers, he recognized that students bring their own practical experience of teaching to interpretation of texts about teaching, challenging the authority of UKOU texts and developing a critical stance (Harris, 1993). Some students may choose not to engage fully with theoretical analysis which does not sit comfortably with day-to-day demands on their practice. But the juxtaposition of theory and practice which distance learning and resource-based learning can offer, creates an enrichment of learning possibilities which evaluation should explore.

Evaluation has also encompassed the social contexts and social status of its students. Walker (1993) for example sees that students for whom course study is interwoven around the tasks and in the locations of daily life, use their everyday experience to interpret what the course is about and the purpose of study. Kirkup and others have focused specifically on the gendered nature of learning, both as this affects course choice and the experience of study (Kirkup, 1989; Ross and Scanlon, 1991; Woodley and Ashby, 1994).

While these studies emphasize demographic participation and success rates, there have also been attempts to raise language use as a factor which has exclusionary effects for some students. The UKOU for example developed an equal opportunities guide to language and image, which countered not only sexist but all forms of language which apparently exclude, belittle or patronize known sectors of its readership. The reaction to this guide included powerful positive and negative responses (Kirkup and Taylor, 1994) which serves to emphasize the point elaborated within this perspective, that the meaning of a course is a contested issue, and one which does not lie in any simple sense in the content of the materials alone.

Woodley has also argued that evaluation should encompass the analysis of student choices and performance across all the modules or courses at each level.

Where this is done, patterns and regularities emerge which provide an important framework for interpreting the feedback on individual modules. At the UKOU, for example, course-based drop-out rates often show an increase after the early years of course presentation up to the end of what is typically an eight-year life or longer (Woodley, 1995). Although in the first year, course materials are often mailed 'just in time' for study, and assignments and study guidance need improvement, it is also known that there is a high degree of course team and tutor attention to the course while it is new. Students also often have to wait for courses to come into presentation, so that the first cohort includes students who are particularly keen to study that course. It may well be therefore that there is a 'halo' effect in the first year which overcomes any weaknesses in presentation and contributes to high retention rates.

Woodley also notes that graduation rates are becoming lower and slower, since the very first intake of all, in 1971. The lower graduation rate of the 1981 intake, for example, is roughly 40 per cent after eight years, compared with 54 per cent for the 1971 intake after eight years. Although the 1981 intake increases to about 45 per cent after 12 years, the catching-up effect is much less noticeable after that. One of the reasons for this marked difference is the lower rates of graduation of those with low and medium qualifications before OU entry, and the fact that there has been an increase in the proportion in both categories, between 1971 and 1981 (Woodley, op. cit, p.357).

Thus the designers of resource-based modules and courses for independent study need to look beyond the once-off results of a single year, and beyond the design features of their own module in isolation. Interpretation of course-based retention and performance statistics needs to take into account the characteristics of students studying the course and their patterns of course choice and performance over several years.

EVALUATION OF LEARNING AND LEARNING ENVIRONMENTS

Developmental testing

Resource-based learning and the application of new technology create new products, whether in the form of printed texts, cassettes, compact discs, video, computer conferencing or a combination of all of these. If we want to find out how these resources are being used and why, evaluation requires detailed qualitative information about learners' experience and perspectives. This has often been found vital in the case of software for example. It is impossible to predict all the bugs in study guides and procedures, and developmental testing prior to widespread use is vital. 'Debugging' has to be based on what happens when a user attempts to work through material in which she or he has had no prior involvement and approaches with the mental set of the student (Zand, 1994).

In-depth qualitative studies of learning

Developmental testing is typically a small-scale enterprise involving perhaps 10 to 20 students, who work through a course or a section of it, and provide detailed feedback on reactions and difficulties. This feedback is required in time to affect the content of the final version of materials and this is often difficult to achieve. But it is also possible to do in-depth research of student learning when materials are being studied in their final version, for credit.

McCracken, for example, carried out a series of interviews of students studying a geology course, in order to explore the development of visualization skills. The development of understanding in geology requires the ability to imagine the three-dimensional rock formation underlying rock outcrops, particularly as shown in two-dimensional format on a geological map. She found that students experienced three related difficulties: visualizing the three-dimensional; relating present day topography to underlying geology; and discriminating between two concepts – anticline and syncline (McCracken and Laurillard, 1994). These difficulties existed even though three-dimensional models and other modifications to course materials had been introduced to resolve them. None the less, it was concluded that the design of course materials could be changed again in various ways, so as to respond to what the study revealed. The objectives, for example, were pitched at a higher level of generality than the study tasks actually required of students. An example of the change suggested was from this:

> Identify simple folds on geological maps from outcrop patterns and the stratigraphic succession

to this:

> Given a plan view geological map, the student will be able to state which geological processes and features indicate whether a fold structure is a syncline or anticline.

The second objective was suggested because it expressed exactly the intellectual task required of the student. The course materials addressed the task only implicitly, and it was suggested that explicit treatment would benefit student learning. Other recommendations were also made about the presentation and sequencing of concepts, the use of graphical representations and animations, advance organizers and definitions which clarified the precise geological meaning of terms such as strike, plunge, valleys, dips and hills, which are in everyday use.

This study was based on in-depth interviews with eight students who provided detailed feedback before and after carrying out a geological mapping task. It demonstrates that, where the demands of a discipline are generally found to be difficult, in-depth qualitative study of a small number of students can provide insights into characteristic difficulties and confusions. Labour-intensive evaluation of this kind can be justified where essential intellectual skills are taught and are generally found to be difficult. Even good materials can be refined and targeted better to achieve goals of this kind.

Peer evaluation

Evaluation never gave an uncomplicated message to the discerning user of its findings, and its input at this stage in our use of new technology can add to the uncertainty rather than resolving it. What might be right for one sub-set of students would clearly not be right for another. It is important that the course team (if there is one) or tutor, do not look to evaluation for a quick-fix solution. The process of interpreting findings is much more likely to be valuable where a spirit of interest in student learning and likely student response has been part of the process of resources production. Teams who operate in this way are enormously helpful because they challenge each other to review their own prejudices about past experience of student learning.

This process is itself part of the evaluation that should be integrated into production of resources. Peer evaluation is vital, even where there is developmental testing, for several reasons. First is the issue of academic excellence. We cannot take for granted that the content of draft materials is in every respect accurate and that the only issue is whether presentation and pacing could be improved. Time and again, commenting by peers identifies the need to develop the *content* in various ways, including corrections to incorrect or otherwise misleading material. Authors are often not writing in areas identical with their own research and, as a result, colleagues can help to refine what is said and ensure that its validity is not in question. An external reader or assessor is also an important mechanism here for ensuring quality, and if there is time and resource to build in such a role, that is a best-practice solution.

Second, students cannot be expected to know that a different way of explaining or presenting something would have resolved their problems, and this is another perspective that peers bring to evaluation of drafts. They bring a collective experience of how similar concepts or skills and technologies have been taught before and with what results. They can compare the approach taken in draft material and pose questions to the author for consideration in the changes required at subsequent draft stage.

LARGE-SCALE EVALUATION OF MATERIALS IN USE

Instructional design has yet to deliver principles which might be applied to the production of materials with predictable results for student learning. Winn (1990) has also argued that we should not look for guidance in this form but return to theories of learning which can be used to generate solutions appropriate to the specific teaching goals concerned. The fact that each teaching occasion is unique in a number of important ways, is a justification for the importance of evaluation as a routine procedure in maintaining the effectiveness and quality of course resources in use.

The focus of evaluations of these kinds is typically on feedback from whole course populations, providing evidence on a course-by-course basis of student use and the extent to which the course objectives have been achieved. Student feedback also tells us, for example, whether our expectations about workload are near or far from experience on the ground. Courses have to be do-able, in the literal sense of hours available for learning, given the credit rating of the course or module.

Empirical data are also vital to knowing who our students are and tracking their choice of modules. We know that students are now diverse in terms of their ages, what they know and can do, what they want from university study and what combinations of modules they select. The idea of 'a student body' whose responses can be accumulated to identify the majority view, is a fiction which has become more misleading rather than less. Access to new technology can polarize along dimensions of age and to some extent gender.

Thus evaluations frequently reveal that there is no simple majority view. What provokes strong reactions from a minority, passes without comment from the rest. Some may find the material too difficult, the rest not, and so on. It is important for those creating materials and making changes to them to understand not only the percentage of responses on particular issues such as difficulty, workload, relevance or interest, but what is behind the response and what drives the diversity between learners of the same materials.

We have evidence of student change over several years of study, in relation to understanding how to study, in conceptualizing learning and in elements of personal orientation, such as confidence and reasons for study (Beaty and Morgan, 1992; Morgan, 1993). These changes are shown to affect how students use course materials, as well as affecting their learning outcomes. Levels of anxiety about unfamiliar or specialist terminology, coping with workload and being proactive about selection of course material, can all be positively affected by the growth of confidence over several courses.

CONCLUSION

The title of this chapter trails the idea of a culture of learning and I have explored this in relation both to the learning that students do and to the learning that teachers need to engage in if they are to use evaluation findings most productively. Evaluation is not a mechanistic process. It requires the evaluated to be prepared to review accepted truths and cherished viewpoints. Even the crushing weight of thousands of student responses from postal surveys may not lead to change, if the academic leaders of courses are not curious about whether their hunches and intuitions have 'paid off' in terms of student interest and engagement.

Organizations live with 'truths' that we feel confident of and so accept as our starting points. For example, we used to take it for granted that courses should have a 'house style' – that the course resources should seem to speak with one voice through a uniform style. The coherence in terms of an overall design for the physical production of a course is still there now. But we have learned that students also value diversity, and that a sense of the identity of the person coming through in their own prose style and textual structure can be more productive for learning than a relentless uniform 'course speak'.

The practical application of new technology has also generated much implicit self-evaluation, as staff move through the decision-making stages of developing a course curriculum and teaching strategy. They reflect intensively on who is likely to take their course and whether they come with sophisticated skills they will want to use, or with a fear of technologies they have yet to experience hands-on. This also projects forward to a curiosity about the effects on students of new technology in courses, and this has generated increased explicit evaluation, at the 'classic' stages of developmental testing prior to release for general student use, and during the first and subsequent years of that use with the target student population.

The importance of evaluation in the context of mediated teaching where learning takes place remote from the direct guidance of a tutor has been well argued elsewhere (Calder, 1994; Thorpe, 1993). This volume offers exemplars in the higher education context of why it is essential to know what use has been made of resources, what the quality of students' experience was, and what reasons students give for their various reactions. What all of this requires however, is a culture of learning – an open-minded audience of teachers in higher education, interested in how their students learn and what stimulates them to learn better. 'No human endeavour can progress, except by chance, without some way of evaluating its performance' (Bok, 1986, p.66).

REFERENCES

Beaty, E and Morgan, A (1992) 'Developing skill in learning', *Open Learning*, 7, 3, 3–11.
Bok, D (1986) *Higher Learning*, Harvard, Mass: Harvard University Press.
Calder, J (1994) *Programme Evaluation and Quality: A comprehensive guide to setting up an evaluation system*, London: Kogan Page.
Chambers, E (1995) 'Course evaluation and academic quality', in Lockwood, F (ed.) *Open and Distance Learning Today*, London: Routledge.
Evans, T (1994) *Understanding Learners in Open and Distance Education*, London: Kogan Page.
Harris, D (1987) *Openness and Closure in Distance Education*, London: Falmer Press.
Harris, D (1993) 'Distance education at the margins', in Evans, T and Nation, D (eds) *Reforming Open and Distance Education* (pp.55–71), London: Kogan Page.
Kirkup, G (1989) 'Equal opportunities and computing at the Open University', *Open Learning*, 4, 1, 3–8.
Kirkup, G and Taylor, L (1994) 'Gender and power: a case study from the UKOU', in Thorpe, M and Grugeon, D (eds) *Open Learning in the Mainstream* (pp.202–16), Harlow: Longman.

Laurillard, D (1995) 'Multimedia and the changing experience of the learner', *British Journal of Educational Technology*, 26, 3, 179–89.

McCracken, J and Laurillard, D (1994) *A Study of Conceptions in visual Representations: A Phenomenographic Investigation of Learning about Geological Maps*, CITE Report No. 196, Milton Keynes: Open University.

Mason, R (1994) *Using Communications Media in Open and Flexible Learning*, London: Kogan Page.

Morgan, A (1993) *Improving Your Students' Learning*, London: Kogan Page.

Ross, S and Scanlon, E (1991) 'Physicists all: or are Open University graduates different?', *Open Learning*, 6, 2, 3–11.

Rowntree, D (1994) *Preparing Materials for Open, Distance and Flexible Learning: An action guide for teachers and trainers*, London: Kogan Page.

Thorpe, M (1993) *Evaluating Open and Distance Learning* (2nd edn), Harlow: Longman.

Thorpe, M (1995) 'Reflective learning in distance education', *European Journal of Psychology of Education*, 10, 2, 153–67.

Walker, R (1993) 'Open learning and the media: transformation of education in times of change', in Evans, T and Nation, D (eds) *Reforming Open and Distance Education: Critical reflections from practice* (pp.15–35), London: Kogan Page.

Wegerif, R (1995) *Collaborative Learning on TLO 94: Creating an online community*, CITE Report No 212, Milton Keynes: Open University and IET.

Whalley, P (1995) 'Imagining with multimedia', *British Journal of Educational Technology*, 26, 3, 190–204.

Winn, W (1990) 'Some implications of cognitive theory for instructional design', *Instructional Science*, 14, 53–69.

Woodley, A (1995) 'A string of pearls? A broader approach to course evaluation' in Lockwood, F (ed.) *Open and Distance Learning Today*, London: Routledge.

Woodley, A and Ashby, A (1994) *Highways and By-ways: Modelling student flows in distance education*, Milton Keynes: Open University and IET.

Zand, H (1994) 'Developmental testing: monitoring academic quality and teaching effectiveness', in Lockwood, F (ed.) *Materials Production in Open and Distance Learning*, London: Paul Chapman.

Chapter 14

Marketing Resources for Learning

Eileen Elliott de Saez

INTRODUCTION

Just like the inventor, the lecturer needs a bank of resources to fund the time, effort and production refinements required for learning resources. And like it or not, the lecturer needs to acquire marketing knowledge and skills to support the development, promotion and distribution of learning resources.

Marketing is about good communication and, fortunately, lecturers are extremely good communicators. The need to communicate in different ways is at the very heart of resource-based learning. Resource-based learning is a philosophy, as well as a product of education's move into the twenty-first century. The traditional methods of teaching and learning in higher education – small groups, tutor-student relations, well-resourced libraries – are fast becoming luxuries. Even if we could afford them still, they are not necessarily the most appropriate or effective approaches to changing societies' needs and learner profiles. Hodgkinson (1994, p.25) predicts a revolution in the individualized nature of traditional learning in higher education: 'wider access, flexible accreditation, and course structure, and personal computer use may only be the beginning of the development of a pattern of truly open learning'.

PREPARING A MARKETING STRATEGY

In order to prepare a marketing strategy, the lecturer needs to consider with care how the learning society is changing. Who might potential students be? What might be affecting them currently and in the future? Different career prospects, different backgrounds, different personalities, different learning strategies will affect the obvious markets.

Where are all the potential learners? In the institutions of further and higher education would be the obvious answer, but are there potential markets elsewhere? The training programmes of many of the big companies are increasingly sophisticated, and learning resource centres are mushrooming. Industrial companies' needs vary enormously. Consider, for example, the very real problem of companies who have employees on permanent night shift. Where line managers are unwilling to release such employees for staff development purposes in production time, those employers and employees may well be appreciative targets of learning resources which can be tackled by independent learners.

Resource-based learning can empower the learner, encourage autonomy and independence and raise self-esteem. Students are taking greater responsibility for their own learning to a degree which is creating a heavy demand for resource-based learning materials. The danger in that kind of pressure is that materials will be produced without careful consideration of students' true needs. Market research, and the collection and evaluation of relevant data and information, will ensure that more appropriate materials are prepared. Market research will also provide the bedrock information which is vital to target selective segments of the market.

The foundations of an effective marketing strategy are based on good information and sound forecasting. Trends need to be identified in the three areas where you will most need marketing expertise:

- within the institution, where a learning resources culture needs to grow so that support is readily forthcoming for developments;

- within the institution's other departments, where awareness and use of specific learning resources needs to be encouraged;

- in the external world, where a range of potential markets needs to be made aware of your product and moved from awareness to use.

How does one begin to build a culture where the concepts of resources for learning are integral to institutional thinking and mission strategies? Evans (1995, p.131) says,

> the first step in building a platform for changes is to identify where the likely resistance will come from [and] it is vital to identify the key individuals who will support the changes and their reasons for doing so.

Common sense? Of course, but then marketing is based on sound principles, it is why marketing works so effectively. There is an adage that 'only 50 per cent of advertising works, only we don't know which 50 per cent'. It is very much tongue-in-cheek; advertising is a comparatively small part of marketing strategy and, anyway, it allows those of us who think we are never affected by advertising to continue in our delusion.

PEST

A clear picture of the environment is a vital prerequisite to marketing planning. Environmental scanning and analysis must be a continuous monitoring process. The uncontrollable variables which affect the education environment and its markets are complex and dynamic; they are the forces which operate in Political, Economic, Social, cultural and Technological contexts. They are known in marketing jargon as PEST, and a PEST analysis should include a review of relevant legislation too. In particular, copyright law, which is not so much hazy as fog-bound, needs attention. Learning resources will almost inevitably include a proportion of copyright-protected material. Equally important is the question of the lecturer's copyright. Does copyright reside in the lecturer or in the institution which employs the lecturer? It is essential to check the terms of contracts, since practices differ from institution to institution.

Copyright in the UK is complex and copyright clearance can be expensive. Often it can be tied in to a scale of charges depending on how many copies are to be distributed, which would have an effect on the price of the end product. There is a useful guide to the main elements of copyright considerations appended to each title in the series produced by the Oxford Centre for Staff Development, *Course Design for Resource-based Learning* (see, for example, Gibbs and Brown, 1994).

SWOT

As a rich and comprehensive picture emerges of environmental trends, your internal situation needs attention too. A marketing audit, or Strengths, Weaknesses, Opportunities and Threats (SWOT) analysis, of your current situation will initially depress you utterly, or busy you with hope. The SWOT analysis must not be based on gut reactions. It should be a careful consideration of resources, likely obstacles and potential for the support of your learning resource activities and production. Undoubtedly, you will have no difficulty in listing weaknesses – time and money will head the list, but a good rule of thumb is to identify at least two strengths for every weakness listed. The expertise and experience of those creating learning resources are real strengths, as are their knowledge of student and learner responses, the institution's need to reduce class contact time, and design capability in the institution. Do not underestimate what you have going for you. Threats often lurk unseen: copyright permissions may not be given or be too expensive, reproduction of the desirable learning environment or facilities may not be possible elsewhere and certainly would be beyond your control.

The learning resource package may include a number of variables or elements which depend upon another supplier and, in today's climate, who can guarantee longevity of companies? You may not be able to rely on the learners to provide necessary materials either. In its early years, the Open University famously had to send out parcels of worms to enable students to carry out a cognitive learning experiment. Other methods of presenting the same information or experience are your competition, and never underestimate the book as competition. Opportunities will often arise out of identifying weaknesses and threats. A shortfall in design expertise might lead to cooperation with local industry. Existing training packages might lead to complementary materials to extend knowledge or resource packages for different levels of approach. The huge take-up of Investors in People programmes opens up all kinds of possibilities: the appetite for training packages and learning resources is voracious.

Do not immediately list sponsorship under opportunities. Sponsorship may be a time-consuming red herring in this area. The educational institution which has provided the context for the innovation and production of the learning resources may well be regarded as the sponsor, but looking for commercial partners needs to be approached with care. There is no great difficulty in seeking sponsorship. You need to identify who might have an interest in or a connection with your area of work and expertise. Companies exist to match those looking for sponsorship with organizations which are seeking sponsorship opportunities. Concentrate on local organizations and companies to begin with; the multinationals are inundated with requests. Remember that you may sink a considerable amount of time and effort into seeking sponsorship for very little return.

Any request for sponsorship should state specifically why commitment is sought and what type of support is needed. Supporting evidence may be attached, but the initial letter should be short, professional and to the point. Be specific about what funding is needed for, not just general support: state if it is for more sophisticated software, design expertise, training, packaging or distribution costs. Be specific too, about the benefits to the sponsor: will their name be on every item or element of the package, is the intended market for the learning resources the same as the market for their own products and services?

Seek background information about your target sponsor. You do not want to be tied into a deal which may later prove to be an embarrassment. Negotiate on numbers to be produced and a time-scale for your contract. You will be in a strong bargaining position if you need more funding as the learning resources prove a success and further developments ensue. Always have written confirmation on decisions and provide your sponsor with regular reports: this is a partnership. Remember that sponsorship does not always have to be in monies. The provision of facilities or technical expertise or handling distribution are equally valuable.

Franchising may be of more interest to you than sponsorship. Another institution may wish to take the package which you have created and customize it to fit their specific needs. You must retain clear authorship identity and decisions must be documented clearly, especially in regard to author control, and a contract drawn up.

A number of educational publishers are amazingly generous in distributing free work books, overhead transparencies, case studies and software to support major texts. They make no stipulations other than an acknowledgement of source material in their use. You cannot afford to be so generous: a learning package with your name on it should be fully authorized by you. What if the franchiser used inferior or out-of-date examples to support a learning concept? What if reproduced materials were of poor quality? Build control of quality and permitted use into any agreement in the early stages. You may not wish the package to be used after a certain date: programming for self-destruction is possible; non-computer materials can carry an instruction, 'not to be used after...' – but also make sure that the provision is in the contract.

Market segments

Opportunities for development will be exciting, but make sure that you have all the relevant information before making strategic decisions. Detailed information about your intended markets is essential. Market segmentation is increasingly sophisticated to ensure that communications and products are relevant and reach their target markets successfully. Undifferentiated or mass-marketing can work, if a product or service has features acceptable to a wide variety of users, but it is less and less common as users make more sophisticated demands and have a higher expectation of tailor-made service (Elliott de Saez, 1993, p.79).

Marketing mixes can be fine-tuned to serve the needs of segments which have similar characteristics, are accessible and are of a viable size for cost-effectiveness. Learners can be segmented by any number of factors: geographically; in or out of institutions; mode of attendance, full/part-time or open learning; age; qualifications; culture; experience; able-bodied or not. The segment must be homogeneous so that the learning resource can be presented and packaged in an appropriate fashion for a particular group.

Demographic segmentation of the market is easily ascertained from existing published information. Psychographic segmentation is much more difficult and will involve market research. A lecturer may know the needs and aspirations of his or her own groups of students in intimate detail, but they will not necessarily match the profile of the wider market. Aren't mature students the same whoever they are? Maybe, but a glance at *Economic Trends*, *Social Trends* or *Regional Trends*, from the UK Central Statistical Office, will show huge variations in regional behaviour, which may well affect the reception and use of your learning resource materials which had been carefully tuned to the needs of your students.

The market for learning resources will not be individual students, however. It will be the institutional and training providers, the lecturers, the librarians, the learning resource directors. These are the segments which need to be addressed, and the benefits which will accrue to them by purchasing and using your package need to be spelt out. Benefit segmentation is a useful tool, as promotional materials can aim at self-recognition and move the segment into desiring the particular benefits. For some examples, look at the bank which is essentially offering one service, but where the benefits of that service are promoted differently to students, young professionals, young marrieds, the retired and, presumably today, lottery winners.

THE FOUR Ps

The marketing mix appropriate for your markets and product will change over time, as the nature of the learning resources change and the markets change. The marketing mix is a key concept in marketing and is the planned package of elements which will support the producer in reaching target markets. Professor Jerome McCarthy (1978) gave us the four Ps of Product, Place, Price and Promotion as essential elements. The four Ps have been added to and refined;

lately Professor Philip Kotler (Mazure, 1991–2) propounded his view that marketing must focus more sharply on the customer and produced a customer mix of four Cs: customer value, cost to the customer (including time and energy), customer convenience and customer communication.

Product

One of the problems in planning the marketing mix for learning resources is that a learning resource is both tangible and intangible, a product and a service. The worksheets, case studies, software are all tangible, but the nature of the learning and any back-up offered in feedback or assessment are wholly intangible in the learner's eyes. The intangible factors will concern the learner as much as the quality of the materials themselves. What kind of feedback is on offer, when, where and how is it available; is there a charge? A kind of after-sales service portfolio needs to be prepared as part of what is being offered.

The product needs to be presented so that its value to the learner customer is evident. Does it provide different information or the same information in a more accessible format? Is it for a specific learner group? Does it provide new, alternative methods of learning? For example, 'The lifting action of a weight lifter on interactive videodisc' (Cubitt *et al.*, 1994, p.95) sounds like an interesting product development. Are assessment methods helpful or is feedback too tardy to be of value? Does the learning involve reflection, does it involve the learner? What changes might be introduced to make the learner a willing participant?

Resource-based learning can be very attractive to the student who finds group participation difficult, for example. David Harris (1993, p.62) describes the nightmare of a group he tutored for an Open University summer school: 'irrevocably cynical and defensive... members disliked each other and me', and the intensive interactions: 'only taught those students more sophisticated immunisation strategies to preserve their world views against the arguments of the course, rather as a spell in prison teaches some inmates better house-breaking techniques'. Learning resources may be aimed at group activities or the individual learner, but the learning resource package which has been constructed to cater for both approaches is not likely to be particularly successful, since peer learning will be an integral part of the former – and how can that be replaced for the individual student?

It is essential to put the target market at the centre of thinking in relation to the production of the learning resources. Hannagan (1992, p.102) provides a useful checklist of six Os which organizations need to take account of when considering the target market:

- Occupants – which individuals constitute the market?
- Object – what does the market wish to buy?
- Occasions – when does the market make purchases?
- Organizations – who is involved in the decision to purchase?
- Objectives – why does the market buy?
- Operations – how does the market buy?

Place

'Place' in marketing-mix terms looks at where and how the product or service is made available and through what distribution channels. Initially the learning resources may have been available solely in the author's department and spreading thereafter to other departments in the institution. Experience of the internal marketing will have taught the necessary lessons of stock control, record-keeping and delivery on promises. Marketing to the wider world magnifies this to the extent it will be necessary to consider the employment of an agent to handle distribution.

Information on and from buyers is invaluable and it is important that such information is collected, collated and acted upon. Enquiries or complaints should be responded to immediately and there needs to be a system in place to deal with them. Research on user satisfaction and data for product life-cycle decisions will be easier if a system is there from day one, beginning with the internal marketing.

Build in a system of controls and cross-checks. If this sounds daunting, remember it is your reputation as well as product quality which is being protected. However good the product, if it arrives late, damaged or incomplete, the overall perception is of a flawed transaction. An enquiry, whether by telephone, fax or Internet, which is met in a tardy or off-hand manner, dilutes user satisfaction with the product. Contacting customers at a reasonable period after purchase to ascertain satisfaction rates is good public relations and sound common sense. It will give good pointers for the future development of the resource materials: amendments, additions, different approaches, and other learning resources needed.

Price

Pricing will depend on a number of factors: cost of materials, design services and distribution; plus promotion costs and overheads. Never underestimate the human resource cost – build in the true costs. Greater numbers produced do not always produce savings. You will need to build in suppliers' predicted cost rises, as well as copyright expenses, which may rise according to numbers produced. Consider joint publishing or publishing in an existing series to reduce costs. Investigate what the market is paying for similar products and consider discounting for early orders, big orders or special groups. Institutional help will be available, take advantage of the advice offered. You may not need or wish to make a profit, but remember it is always more attractive to bring a price down than push it up later.

Promotion

Promotion ranges from making sure that learning resources are on the agenda of every relevant committee to expensive, professionally produced advertising.

Public relations forms an important part of promotion strategy, but never think that PR is a cheap alternative to paid-for advertising. Public relations needs strategic planning, is hugely time-consuming in preparation and execution, and needs financial resources too.

Personal selling is very effective, and academic standing and academic contacts will ensure a ready market once the education world is aware of what is on offer. That raising of awareness is vital to draw attention to work in progress as well as the finished product. Write about your work; the full-blooded academic paper is not always necessary, and many academic journals accept short 'bulletin-board' pieces. Offer to do workshops, as well as delivering papers, at conferences. Consider poster activities at conferences. Organize your own workshops or training days and introduce the new product.

Think about press releases and seek advice from the institute's press officer. It will be necessary to provide the titles of journals which your target market reads. Remember the media can make what they will of your press release: you are merely sending them information, which they are entitled to use, amend or reject. However, editors have acres of space to fill and a press release, well produced in physical format as well as content, will receive due attention. You may intend to produce your own press releases and it is not difficult, but it is time-consuming. You need to identify what is the most effective time for your market to be alerted to the product and to make sure that your press release will arrive in due time for appropriate issues of the relevant journals. Use your own teaching experience as a guide. When do you catch up on reading, when do you plan courses for the next academic year, when do you order/purchase materials?

Use decent stationery: a many-folded, tissue-thin sheet of paper will be consigned to the bin, and remember to use the Internet too if you are a confident user. Identify the source of the press release immediately and obviously; if it is your department rather than the institution, make that absolutely clear. There may be a publishing arm to your institution which will deal with distribution, but the press release is aimed at creating awareness and arousing interest, so the source needs to be where further information may be sought. Give your press release a title: a short simple title, not a headline – the journalists will do that. Answer the question, what is this about, to give you your title.

All sub-editors will look for what is new, different, unique, improved, fresh. Give it to them in the first few words of your text. There are thousands of ways of saying first, changed, innovative, etc; 'new' is still the most effective way of catching attention. Answer the questions, what, why, how, who, how much and when available, briefly, but without resorting to telegram style. Try to keep the text to one side of A4; if you create sufficient interest they will contact you for more information. A quote from a named person, including their job title or status, is a very useful aid to ensuring that the press release is used. When published it looks as if the journalists have been out and about interviewing, so it's useful to them. Finally, add a contact name, status and telephone number for further information and ensure that the named person is prepared to answer questions from the media – being interviewed live on radio does not come easily to all. The marketing model you are aiming at is AIDA: awareness – interest – desire – action.

You need to create awareness of your learning resources and provoke your target market into being sufficiently interested in what you are offering to the point of actually wanting the resources. You also need to provided your potential buyers with appropriate and easy-to-use ways of obtaining your learning resources. For example, use reply cards or coupons which can be accepted as official orders or provide telephone numbers, fax numbers or Internet addresses where orders may be taken.

The teeming markets of the education world are waiting!

REFERENCES

Cubitt, J *et al.* (1994) 'A flexible learning strategy for design and technology students'. in Wade, W *et al.* (eds) *Flexible Learning in Higher Education* (pp.89–98), London: Kogan Page.

Elliott De Saez, E (1993) *Marketing Concepts for Libraries and Information Services*, London: Library Association Publishing.

Evans, I (1995) *Marketing for Schools*, London: Cassell.

Gibbs, G and Brown, S (1994) *Course Design for Resource-based Learning: Built environment*, Oxford Centre for Staff Development.

Hannagan, T J (1992) *Marketing for the Non-profit Sector*, London: Macmillan.

Harris, D (1993) 'Distance education at the margins', in Evans, T and Nation, D (eds) *Reforming Open and Distance Education* (pp.55–71), London: Kogan Page.

Hodgkinson, K (1994) 'Flexible provision for student diversity', in Wade *et al.*, op. cit.

Mazure, L (1991-2) 'Silent satisfaction (an interview with Professor Philip Kotler)', *Marketing Business*, December–January, 24–7.

McCarthy, E J (1978) *Basic Marketing: A managerial approach* (6th edn), Homewood, Ill.: Richard D Irwin.

Chapter 15

Conclusions

Sally Brown and Brenda Smith

We conclude this book with some salutary tales for those who wish to implement resource-based learning and some positive thoughts to encourage those embarking on this route.

TELL THEM WHAT YOU'RE DOING AND WHY!

Problems can arise when briefing sessions on the reasons for introducing and using resource-based learning are omitted or are unconvincing. In a letter in *The Guardian* education section, 12 March 1996, a disgruntled parent, under the heading 'Undirected Study', wrote:

> I was shocked and dismayed when I was sent details by my son of a plan to halve the teaching time in his second year.... It's very expensive to keep a child at university these days and it does not seem right that a university can unilaterally impose a 50% cut in services on what is a captive market. To make matters worse, the published information sheet tries to persuade students that they will be better off because they will have more time to work on their own (ludicrously labelled 'directed study'). If this has been caused by government policy, why can't we be told, and we can then take this into account when voting in the forthcoming election.

It is obvious here that the message had not got through to the student or the parents. Had the university concerned run proper briefing and training sessions? Or had they left themselves wide-open to criticisms that the only purpose of introducing resource-based learning was to save money? Where could students and parents see the added value of the new curriculum delivery strategy?

PLAY IT SAFE

In another incident we heard about, a university spent a lot of time and money creating learning resources for a department, ensuring that consistency was achieved by producing documentation on a single machine used by one admin-

148

istrator. The work was backed up on floppies, but when burglars broke in they took them as well as the computer, as they were stored alongside. Six months' work was wasted, as some of the originals from which the workbooks had been created had been destroyed.

Resource-based learning materials are both extremely valuable and vulnerable. Course teams need to be sure that their resource material is secure against theft, malicious damage, fire or other disaster. They need to ask whether they are over-reliant on a single individual to produce materials, so that effective curriculum delivery is at risk if that person leaves or is off sick long-term.

NEVER MIND THE QUALITY, FEEL THE VELOCITY!

Stories abound of materials being produced with the wrong logos, serious typographical errors, author's or co-author's names being omitted, incorrectly sequenced pages and diagrams left out or printed in the wrong places. Resource-based learning materials are often produced at speed and errors are easily made in the process. Course materials that arrive halfway through the study period are not unheard of even in the best organizations.

People find materials which are full of errors and which don't do what they promise a barrier to effective learning. Teams need to ask how good their quality assurance mechanisms are. Have enough time and resources been built in to check the production quality? Is there someone looking at materials at final proof stage who comes with a fresh eye and who isn't so close to the material that errors are allowed to creep through? Whose responsibility is it that the work is absolutely right before expensive copying processes are put into motion?

DATED AND DANGEROUS

Some of the most disheartening stories relate to the situation where a substantial investment has been made to produce first-class learning resources but none has been set aside for revision and reproduction. In some instances, there is just not enough money available to reprint perfectly good resource material. In others, no staff time is allowed for the inevitable redrafting after the first run of a course, so the materials soon become dated. Another problem is when large print runs are produced to get a cheaper reprographics rate, but they are badly stored, so students get materials that are grubby or faded. Even sadder is when excellent materials are produced to run on equipment that becomes obsolete before the materials themselves have become outdated.

All these are expensive and largely avoidable errors. Resource-based learning producers need to check whether they have built a maintenance and upgrade cycle into the planning of curriculum materials. How good is the production team's forward planning? Have appropriate budgets been allocated to ensure that materials will continue to be usable? Are there mechanisms in place to ensure that evaluation can lead to enhancement?

'NOT MADE HERE' EQUALS 'NO GOOD'

If a university decides to use bought-in learning resources, it is important that the academics using them are fully convinced of their value. It has been known for a lecturer to make disparaging remarks to students about the value of an element of a learning package, with the result that students lost confidence and interest in the materials as a whole.

Course teams using resource-based learning need to be quite clear about why and how they are using externally produced packages. If the package as a whole does not provide a perfect fit with the needs of the students, it may be necessary to produce supplementary learning guides to accompany the original materials, and to provide local contextualization.

GETTING IT RIGHT

Packages are sometimes made available to students using technology to which not all of them have access, because they cannot get onto networks, don't have the right computer or because their hardware has the wrong kind of configuration for the particular software. Problems also arise when students experience disasters with machines breaking down, getting stolen or being over-booked.

It is extremely difficult to avoid such problems completely, but the organizing team would do well to 'walk through' the use of learning packages on computers before students are actually asked to use them, so that there is a chance to ask the 'What happens if...' questions. It is also useful if a helpline facility can be made available for students in trouble with their IT.

DELIVERING RESOURCE-BASED LEARNING

Resource-based learning is here to stay as one of the means we have available for course delivery. The word 'delivery' is often used in this context as if learning was something that could be delivered like a parcel. We prefer instead to see the term used in the sense of bringing something into the world, as a baby is 'delivered'. It is hard work, has a long lead-time, always involves more than one person, often works well if a back-up team with professional expertise is available, can require specialist intervention when things go wrong, may involve blood, sweat and tears, represents a beginning rather than a finished process, can have effects for a very long time and people frequently swear they will never do it again (but often do)!

Using resource-based learning for course delivery can, however, have tremendously high pay-offs: it can enhance the learning process, provide great benefits for students and staff, and can encourage students to develop abilities that will lead them to become lifelong learners. We wish you every success.

Index